Daily
Groove

How to
Enjoy Parenting...
Unconditionally!

by

Scott Noelle

The Daily Groove
How to Enjoy Parenting... Unconditionally!

Scott Noelle
PO Box 19901
Portland, OR 97280
USA

Website: www.enjoyparenting.com

Cover photos:

1	2	3	4
5			6
7			8
9			10
11	12		13

1. *(L to R)* Willow, Beth, and Olivia Noelle; photo by Scott Noelle.
2. Emily and Seth Troper; photo by Michael Troper.
3. Lisa and Emily Biskup; photo by Don Stromberg.
4. *Anonymous*
5. Carlos, Veronica, and Ariel Miros; photo by Pablo F. Sopuerta.
6. Lorraine and Chloe Faehndrich; photo by Jennifer Arnold-Delgado.
7. Nam-Ha and Kobe-Li Quach; photo by Hayley Quach.
8. Liam and Lloyd Hubbard; photo by Laura Joyce-Hubbard. (www.mothergoosephotography.com)
9. *Anonymous*
10. Laban and Neige Christenson; photo by Steven Christenson.
11. Krista Cornish Scott; photo by Brett Cornish Scott.
12. Eli, Avery, Michael, Lisa, and Emily Biskup; photo by Don Stromberg.
13. Willow and her grandmother Amy; photo by Scott Noelle.

Cover design and book design by Scott Noelle.

ISBN: 145375721X   EAN-13: 9781453757215

For my family...

Beth, Olivia & Willow

Acknowledgments

My heart is overflowing with appreciation and gratitude for the many wonderful people — family, friends, teachers, clients, and readers — who've inspired and supported me on my path. Your wisdom, love, and generosity are invested in these pages. I especially wish to thank...

~ My parents, Amy and Peter, who've always encouraged me to follow my dreams.

~ Tom Blaylock and Jim Samuels, whose mentoring in my youth taught me the true meaning of empowerment.

~ The many authors whose books have shaped my views, especially Richard Bach, Ron Smothermon, Daniel Quinn, Ann Weiser Cornell, Joseph Chilton Pearce, Alfie Kohn, E Richard Sorenson, Gordon Neufeld, Esther and Jerry Hicks, and...

~ Jean Liedloff, whose book, *The Continuum Concept*, blew my mind and set me on this path.

~ Emily and Michael Troper, Heidi Petrino, and Ingrid Bauer, who've been extraordinarily supportive, year after year.

~ Michelle Mersy and Traci Nelson for their feedback and proofreading assistance.

~ The joyful parents and children whose photos grace the cover of this book (listed on page ii).

And last but not least, my beloved partner Beth — and our children/teachers, Willow and Olivia — who inspired many of the ideas in this book and held the vision with me every step of the way...

I am truly blessed!

PART I

Introduction: How to Enjoy Parenting

Introduction: How to Enjoy Parenting 1

The Law of Attraction 2

"Good Vibrations" 4

The Creative Pleasure Principle 5

Emotions as Inner Guidance 6

Unconditionality 7

Partnership 9

Attachment & Bonding 10

Parenting with Authentic Power 11

    The Power of Acceptance 12

    The Power of Alignment 12

    The Power of Attunement 13

    The Power of Attraction 13

    The Power of Attachment 14

    The Power of AND 14

    The Power of Appreciation 15

A Personal Transformation 15

Putting the Principles Into Practice 16

PART II: The Daily Groove 19

Finding Your Groove...
  One Day at a Time........................20
Idealism vs. Perfectionism..............21
Merging With Your Child's Flow.......22
Let Your Love Shine........................23
Be Self/Centered............................24
Growing Down................................25
Resistance Is Futile.........................26
Be Selective... Go Shopping! 27
Go With the Flow...
  Even If It's 'Wrong'.......................28
Helping vs. Co-creation...................29
Have a NICE day! 30
"I'd Rather Feel Good!"...................32
Beyond Right and Wrong................33
Say Yes FIRST................................34
Mother Nature Always Says YES! 35
Invisible Teaching...........................36
"What Happened?!"........................37
Your Emotional Guidance................38
Be Unreasonable............................40
Boycott That Thought! 41
"What's GOOD about that?".............42
Unconditionality vs. Desires............43
Inner Freedom Feels Good...............44
Who's Demanding?.........................45
The Joy of Being Known..................46
The Joy of NOT Being Known..........47
Creator, or Reactor?.......................48
The Play Ethic................................49
Say YES to Desire...........................50
What Is "YES-Energy"?....................51
Red Light, Green Light....................52
No Regrets.....................................53
Not Wrong.....................................54
The Joy of Manipulation..................55
The Big Lie.....................................56
Love Train......................................57
Acceptance vs. Tolerance................58
Interpret Your Way to Partnership....59
Rethinking Consistency...................60
Riding Coattails..............................61
Protectiveness vs. Trust..................62
The Power of Attraction..................63
The Absolute Value of Your Child....64
Transcending Culture......................65
The Benefit of the Doubt.................66
Making Peace With What Is.............67

The Power of an Open Heart...........68
The Now Game...............................69
"Because" vs. "Be Cause"................70
"Because I Said So!"........................71
Transforming Anger........................72
The Freedom Paradox.....................75
Balance vs. Bigness.........................76
The Wild Child...............................77
The Power of Silence......................78
An Unconditional Icebreaker...........79
Weird Is Good! 80
Easing Exhaustion from Within........81
"Do-Over!"....................................82
Going Along for the Ride.................83
Love the Behavior, Too...................84
Don't Explain.................................85
Rich With Desire............................86
Invisible Abundance.......................88
Swashbuckling Through
  Parenthood.................................89
Needs and Desires..........................90
Desires Are More Attractive............92
The Power of AND..........................93
Positive Apology............................94
Kids Hear Your Vibe,
  Not Your Words..........................95
The (Real) Magic Word...................96
The 51% Principle...........................97
FEEL Your Way to Find Your Way......98
Implicit Validation..........................99
Nothing but Roses.........................100
Generalizing Desires......................101
Be Real...102
There is only YES...........................103
The Joy of Sharing.........................104
A Human Becoming........................105
Unconditional Presence:
  The Oak Tree..............................106
No Consequences...........................107
Why?...108
Emotional Midwifery......................109
Get In a Receiving Mode................110
Hindsight In Foresight....................112
Healthy Selfishness........................113
Confidently Uncertain....................114
The Shadow of a Doubt..................115

HOLIDAY GROOVES
  For the New Year:
    Remember Your Purpose......116
  For Valentine's Day:
    The Love Game....................117
  Every Day Is Mother's Day! 118
  Independence Day for
    (R)evolutionary Parents.........119
  For Halloween:
    Matters of Life and Death.....120
  For Election Day:
    Creative Democracy.............121
  A Post-Modern Thanksgiving.....122
  Part-Time Santa,
    Full-Time Visionary...............123
Love Notes to Myself.....................124
Feeling Good vs. Being "Right".......125
Two Kinds of Responsibility...........126
Relieving Time Pressure................127
From REactive to PROactive...........128
Seeing the Forest for the Trees......129
Life Is Messy... Get Over It! 130
What Makes Kids So Wonderful?.....131
WWCD: What Would a Child Do?.....132
Patience vs. Presence....................133
PREsponsive Parenting..................134
WordWatch: Always/Never.............135
Goodness Is Inspired, Not Required...136
"I Didn't Sign Up For This!"............137
The Cast Party............................138
Driving With the Brakes On...........139
The Creative Pleasure Principle......140
Pleasure-oriented Parenting..........141
WordWatch: Should/Shouldn't.......142
The Oxygen Mask Rule..................143
Fire Drill! 144
Falling In Love for the
  First Time... Again....................145
The Power of Humility..................146
Children ALWAYS Cooperate.........147
Unreasonable Love.......................148
Blessing the Mirror......................149
WordWatch: My...........................150
Letting Go of HOW.......................151
Your Portable Comfort Zone..........152
Say Goodbye to Guilt....................153
Infinite Love................................154
The One-Body Principle.................155
Your Heart's Desire.......................156
The Body Scan.............................157

Practicing For Peace......................158
Rethinking Sociality......................159
No Problem! 162
"I Want It NOW!"...........................163
The Sticky Speedometer................164
Ignore the Score...........................165
Detoxifying Parental Guilt.............166
You "Should" Follow Your Bliss! 167
Time-In..168
Why Kids Lie................................170
Seeing Eye to Eye.........................171
"Scare City"..................................172
Pushing Buttons...........................173
The Power of Story........................174
"I'm Not a Frog-Boiler!"..................176
The Appreciation Game.................177
Jump for Joy! 178
Taking Children Seriously..............179
The Choosing Ritual......................180
Authentic Pleasure Is Priority One.....182
Are You Your Child's Friend?.........183
The Roots of Violence...................184
The Trickle-Down Theory
  of Human Kindness...................185
The Path of Least Resistance.........186
Are You Resisting Resistance?........187
Inner Separation Anxiety...............188
WordWatch: "Don't..."...................190
Beyond DOs and DON'Ts...............191
DARE to Be Real! 192
Contraction vs. Expansion.............193
The Look......................................194
Truth Is Overrated........................195
Worry Less, Love More..................196
The Perspective Game...................197
Is Joy Knocking On Your Door?......198
Power Is Your Friend.....................199
The Power of Intention..................200
"I Feel Like Screaming!".................201
Small Body, Big Spirit....................202
The Power of Inner Freedom..........203
The Canary In the Coal Mine..........204
Soccer Field Parenting...................205
Terrible Two's and
  Rebellious Teens... NOT! 206
The Myth of Fairness.....................208
Unadulterated Fun........................209
Leading-edge Parenting
  Requires Faith............................210

Appendices

A. The Art of Unconditionality.......................211

B. Getting More Support..................................217

C. Alphabetical List of "Grooves"....................218

Part

Introduction:

How to Enjoy Parenting

The Daily Groove is based on a radical premise:

Mother Nature intended parenting to be FUN!

That perspective doesn't get much airtime in our culture. Sure, we say that children are a blessing, and we mean it, but that only seems to justify the hard work and personal sacrifice that parenting presumably requires.

Well, what if it's *not* supposed to be hard work? What if it could be *really* easy? What if your parenting actually gets better the more you relax and *enjoy* it? And what if you could enjoy parenting in spite of the problems of society, a troubled childhood, or any other adverse conditions?

As you read and apply the ideas in this book, you'll begin to discover that all of the above are true! You can transform the daily *grind* of parenthood into a daily *groove* that's deeply satisfying and feels good most of the time.

Throughout these pages, I encourage you to approach parenting in a creative, empowering, pleasure-oriented way. Authentic power and pleasure are naturally *attractive* to children and parents alike, so this approach creates a positive feedback loop: it makes everyone want more!

Attraction-based parenting eliminates the "need" for conventional, control-oriented, fear-based parenting. If you've resorted to coercive parenting tactics out of sheer frustration, this approach will restore your faith in human nature. You will come to know with certainty that *children are innately good*, and their goodness can be fostered *joyfully* through unconditional love and creative partnership.

The Law of Attraction

Many of the parenting strategies in this book are based on a unique, practical interpretation of the *Law of Attraction*.

Simply put, the Law of Attraction is the idea that "like attracts like." In practical terms, it means that *whatever you focus on tends to expand in your experience.* Whatever you pay attention *to*, you get more *of.*

Consider, for example, how people with similar interests gravitate toward each other at a party. An interest is a tendency to think about and pay attention to a particular subject. If you're interested in nutrition, your ears will perk up when someone mentions a buzzword like "organic," and you'll be attracted to that conversation — even more so if the person talking looks and dresses like the people who frequent your favorite health food store. Your eyes and ears are *attuned* to that subject, so you're *attracted* to interactions that make it a bigger part of your life.

Beliefs and expectations are also patterns of thought that shape our experiences. Someone who expects the party to be boring will be unconsciously attracted to people who meet that expectation, while someone who expects to have fun will be attracted to others with the same intentions. One will say, "That was the *worst* party ever!" while the other will say, "That was the *best* party ever!" Each of them "creates their own reality" because each of them has a different perspective of Reality. Thus, you "attract" experiences that match your thoughts, whether you're thinking about what you *want* or what you *don't want*.

The Law of Attraction, as described above, is consistent with conventional psychology. Most of the experiences you attract can be explained in terms of beliefs, perceptions, expectations, and behaviors. But when the phrase "Law of Attraction" was coined by esoteric writers over a century ago, it referred to a *spiritual* principle that explained subtle phenomena such as creativity, synchronicity, and other mysteries that defied material explanation. To them, the Law of Attraction was part of a growing movement to integrate science and spirituality.

Today, that movement is growing more rapidly than ever, and in this book I encourage you to take part in it by including both perspectives — material *and* spiritual. If you have a preference for one or the other, I invite you make room for both points of view as you consider the ideas in this book. See what happens when you let your rational and intuitive sides play together!

"Good Vibrations"

When you hear phrases like "that resonates with me," "we're in tune with each other," and "this place has a good vibe," that's the Law of Attraction at play. Such phrases are common because we intuitively sense what science is only beginning to understand: *everything* is essentially *energy in vibration* — not only physical energies such as light, sound, and matter, but also subtle energies like thoughts and "life force." These are all *vibrational* phenomena.

So another way to say "like attracts like" is that vibrationally similar things are drawn together. This tendency is evident throughout nature: birds attract each other with their songs (sound vibration), flowers attract bees with their colors (light vibration), mammals attract mates through scent (molecular vibration), etc.

Children are particularly sensitive to the emotional states, or "vibes," of their parents. These are communicated through sight (as "body language") and sound (as vocal tone and inflection), and more subtly through thought vibrations and even through the electromagnetic fields generated by our hearts. When you're stressed, your child can sense the "bad vibes," which s/he may reflect and amplify as increasing fussiness or irritability. If you're stressed *about* your child's reactions, it forms a vicious cycle of increasing stress. Fortunately, it works both ways: when you emanate "good vibes" around children — that is, when you feel confident, centered, and present — you make it easier for them to connect with their intrinsic Well-Being.

Another phenomenon that can be understood in terms of vibration and attraction is *creativity*. Imagine that thoughts are like radio signals and your mind is like a radio receiver. There may be hundreds of signals permeating the space around your receiver, each vibrating at a specific frequency, but you hear a particular radio station only when your receiver is *tuned* to its frequency. Likewise, you can attract creative ideas by "tuning" your mind to the "frequency" of your desire. This book includes many techniques for enhancing your creativity and becoming more *receptive* to inspiration.

The Creative Pleasure Principle

If you've ever tried tuning a radio to a weak signal and finally gotten the station to come in clearly, you know the feeling of satisfaction you get from *alignment*. A similar feeling arises when you meet someone whose values are in alignment with yours, when you suddenly "get" a joke, or when you find a new pair of shoes that fit perfectly. In fact, there's no form of pleasure that's not in some way the result of alignment — physical, mental, and/or spiritual.

Consider the simple pleasure of biting into a delicious apple. The molecules of the apple are in "vibrational alignment" with your sweet-sensing taste buds, and your body experiences this life-serving alignment as physical pleasure. Your belief that the apple is nutritious is in alignment with your desire for a healthy body, which gives you a kind of "mental pleasure." And when you're fully present to the experience, you align with your Inner Knowing that life is good and all is well, producing the spiritual pleasure of profound appreciation and gratitude.

*By redefining pleasure as **the experience of coming into
alignment**, and applying that definition to every aspect and
level of existence — from the tiniest particle to the fully
developed human being — you begin to see that we are
literally made **of** pleasure, **by** pleasure, and **for** pleasure.*

You also begin to see that our culture's devaluation of
pleasure and glorification of suffering contradict our
deepest nature. Sigmund Freud perpetuated this contra-
diction with his concept of the *pleasure principle*. To Freud,
our innate pleasure orientation was a liability to be overcome — a savage instinct to seek immediate gratification
regardless of the broader consequences. But as you apply
the ideas in this book, you'll discover that your whole
family can be pleasure-oriented in ways that are deeply
satisfying for everyone, both immediately *and* in the Big
Picture. I use the term *Creative Pleasure Principle* to dis-
tinguish this perspective from the Freudian view and to
acknowledge the vital role of pleasure (alignment) in the
creative process.

Emotions as Inner Guidance

The Creative Pleasure Principle gives you a new way to
understand emotions in terms of alignment:

> *Your emotions indicate the degree of alignment
> between your active thoughts and your Authentic Self.*

Your *Authentic Self* is your spiritual essence, or "Who You
Really Are" — a being of Pure Love who is connected to
infinite Well-Being. When you look at newborn babies, it's
easy to see that they are Pure Love. The babies know it, too,
but most babies eventually forget Who They Really Are.

They acquire thoughts, beliefs, and perceptions that are out of alignment with their Authentic Self. It happens to virtually everyone in our culture.

Fortunately, you can use your emotions to guide your thinking into alignment with your Authentic Self. The greater the alignment, the better you feel, and your improved feelings indicate that you're *attracting* your authentic desires.

With this understanding, you can appreciate the value of your child's "negative" emotions — and your own, too. They are helpful indicators of a need for inner alignment. Getting into alignment with your Self — also called *centering* — makes you catalyst for your child's inner alignment. And since alignment is a source of pleasure, centered parenting feels less like work and more like play — just as Mother Nature intended.

Unconditionality

If authentic pleasure is consistently guiding us toward Well-Being, why are we stressed out so much of the time?

The problem is that we've been trained to ignore our Inner Guidance and connect with Well-Being *conditionally.* In other words, we expect to feel good *only* under certain conditions, including conditions that are difficult to control, like the weather or other people's behavior and opinions. We've been "conditioned" to feel bad when unwanted conditions arise.

I call this way of thinking *conditionality.* The primary effect of conditionality is disempowerment, because it reinforces the belief that external conditions have the power to *make* you happy or unhappy. Conditionality leads you to pursue happiness by constantly *controlling* conditions, including others' behavior — an overwhelming and impossible task that leads to stress, exhaustion, and burnout.

You can free yourself from control games and reclaim your Authentic Power by cultivating *un*conditionality, which I define as *the willingness to allow Well-Being into your experience, regardless of external conditions.**

Unconditionality is the basis of unconditional love. As you develop this inner skill, you realize that there is essentially no difference between unconditional love for your child and unconditional love for yourself.

The paradoxical nature of unconditionality will blow your mind! For example, you will often find that conditions change to your liking as soon as you make peace with conditions as they are.

When you practice unconditionality, you will go out of agreement with those who are still entrenched in conditionality. When you are not upset about things that upset them, they'll think you don't care. Conditional parents will misinterpret your unconditional love as "permissiveness." You will have to choose between being "right" (by their standards) and *feeling good*.

Just know that when you trust your Inner Guidance and choose to "follow your bliss," others will eventually notice that while they're stressing about conditions, you're enjoying life unconditionally. Someday they will thank you for showing them that Well-Being is never more than a thought away.

* See also *The Art of Unconditionality* on page 211.

Partnership

Most spiritual traditions speak of a divine Oneness that transcends, but also includes, all things — the One that manifests as the many. This One-as-many paradox is embodied in *partnership*. In partnership we experience both unity *and* individuality. When you're in alignment with your Self, and your child is in alignment with his or her Self, you can easily align with each other and experience the pleasure of authentic partnership.

The structure of the material world is essentially one of partnership. Atoms form partnerships called molecules; molecules form partnerships called cells; cells form partnerships called bodies; bodies form partnerships called families; and so on. Complex ecosystems, like rainforests and coral reefs, are intricate tapestries of partnerships. Every part of the system is brought into alignment with every other part by the Law of Attraction, and every partnership is sustained by (and for) pleasure — the flow of Life Energy that arises from their alignment. Even natural "enemies" such as the lion and the gazelle are partners, although the benevolence of such partnerships is difficult to see through the lens of our culture.

The human species evolved within this context of partnership, giving rise to human cultures that were primarily pleasure- and partnership-oriented. But during the last ten thousand years (a blip on the evolutionary time scale), most human cultures shifted into a mode of living and thinking that emphasized *domination* rather than partnership. Domination is seeking power *over* others while partnership is experiencing Authentic Power *with* others.

Biologically, every human baby born today is nearly identical to our ancient ancestors who evolved in a partnership-oriented environment. In other words, children are born *expecting* to be in partnership with their parents. A newborn nursling's instinctive rooting reflex is an expectation the mother's partnership in feeding. The natural tendency of children to emulate their parents' behavior is an expectation of their parents' partnership in modeling. These and other innate expectations are violated when parents sacrifice partnership to enforce the expectations of the dominator culture.

By restoring the natural partnership of parents and children, we are also contributing to a broader cultural shift toward conscious, creative partnership in all human affairs.

Attachment & Bonding

When a parent-child partnership unfolds naturally, both parent and child form a strong desire to be physically and emotionally close to each other. Psychologists call this *secure attachment* and *affectional bonding.*

The ideas in this book work especially well in conjunction with *Attachment Parenting*, an approach that honors our attachment instincts and promotes secure attachment through responsive nurturing, especially with babies and younger children. Most parents who practice Attachment Parenting describe it in terms of *doing*: babywearing, breast-feeding, co-sleeping, etc. This book emphasizes the parent's state of *being* — the "inner game" of parenting.

What you do as a parent makes a difference to your child, but no amount of *doing* can overcome the effects of *being* out of alignment. Parents who go through the motions of Attachment Parenting but are still under the influence of the dominator culture will be disappointed if they expect their actions alone to produce happy, securely attached children. *Healthy attachment is sustained by mutual attraction, which arises from inner alignment.* When you're in alignment with your Authentic Self, you become very attractive to your child. You radiate that which your child desires above all else: unconditional love and a feeling of confidence that All Is Well.

If you're at a place on your parenting path where you're feeling disconnected from your child, take comfort in the fact that you don't have to achieve perfect alignment to restore secure attachment and bonding. No matter how far out of alignment you've gone, you can start where you are and come into alignment at your own pace. Children are amazingly resilient, and human nature is on your side: coming into alignment always feels good.

Parenting with Authentic Power

The dominator tactics of conventional parenting are never truly empowering, but the partnership approach gives you the real thing: a deep connection to Authentic Power. You can create a powerful parent–child partnership using...

The Power of **Acceptance**
The Power of **Alignment**
The Power of **Attunement**
The Power of **Attraction**
The Power of **Attachment**
The Power of **AND**
The Power of **Appreciation**

You can access any of these seven powers at any time, but often they unfold more-or-less sequentially, over a period of days, hours, minutes, or even seconds. The following descriptions will help you understand this process. Each description includes examples of thoughts that you can use to activate that particular power.

The Power of Acceptance

The more you can accept (be at peace with) life conditions as they are, the less they have power over you. Accepting *what is* (including your child's unwanted behavior and your own perceived shortcomings) allows you to stop resisting and start aligning with your authentic desires.

> EMPOWERING THOUGHTS: "Even though I don't like this [condition, behavior, emotion, etc.], I can accept that it's *what is*." "It's okay to be *here* on our way to where we're going." "I could let go and choose peace." "In the big picture, All Is Well."

The Power of Alignment

As your thoughts, beliefs, perspectives, and interpretations come into alignment with your Authentic Self, stress subsides and you feel relief or pleasure. Your state of inner peace and pleasure then makes you a catalyst for your child's inner alignment.

> EMPOWERING THOUGHTS: "I'd rather feel good than be 'right'." "There must be a better-feeling way to think about this." "My emotions are guiding me into alignment with my Self."

The Power of Attunement

Acceptance and alignment increase your capacity for empathic connection, or attunement, with your child. When you're attuned, you have a better sense of what your child is experiencing, which makes you more responsive and enhances the sense of partnership between you and your child.

> EMPOWERING THOUGHTS: "My child and I are both connected to the same Source." "I am willing to see my child's point of view, feel how it feels, *and* stay connected to my knowing that All Is Well."

The Power of Attraction

When you're attuned with your child and aligned with your Authentic Self, your child is naturally attracted to you — s/he wants to be closer to you and gradually becomes interested in what pleases you. This attraction leads to greater alignment and attunement, which further amplifies the attraction. It's a positive feedback loop that culminates in a strong, healthy attachment.

> EMPOWERING THOUGHTS: "I can enjoy parenting without resorting to threats, punishments, rewards, or any form of coercion." "The power of attraction is strong enough to pull us into alignment with each other's desires."

The Power of Attachment

When your child is securely attached to you, s/he is less inclined to seek the (false) security one gets from trying to control conditions and others' behavior. Securely attached children tend to be more willing to flex and go with your flow. Your life flows more easily when you consciously make yourself more "attachable" by attending to your inner alignment and staying attuned to your child.

> EMPOWERING THOUGHTS: "The quality of our relationship is more important than how my child behaves." "Unconditional love is the basis of a healthy attachment."

The Power of AND

When your desires seem to be in conflict with your child's desires, you can unleash your creativity by "AND-ing" the desires: affirming that there must be some way that both you *and* your child can be satisfied, and aligning with that thought until an inspired solution arises. AND encourages *healthy selfishness* as you discover that win/win outcomes are not only possible, they are far more satisfying than win/lose outcomes. The power of AND helps you build a stronger partnership with your child.

> EMPOWERING THOUGHTS: "I may not know *how* we can both be satisfied, but I know there must be a way." "There are always more possibilities than I can see."

The Power of Appreciation

Appreciation brings out the best in everyone. As you form the habit of being appreciative, you not only transform your own life but also the lives of everyone you touch, especially your children. When you appreciate *unconditionally*, you create value from Nothing. There is nothing more empowering than to give and receive love for no reason other than your desire to create a more loving world.

> EMPOWERING THOUGHTS: "Everything that happens in my life contributes to my well-being in some way." "Every shadow makes the Light appear more beautiful." "It's ALL good." "I love life!"

ℰↄ ↄℰ

Once you've internalized the concepts and principles in this book, you can use these seven powers to transform stressful parenting situations into positive experiences. Simply recalling the "seven A's" one at a time and thinking about how each one applies to the situation is often all it takes to get you back in your groove.

A Personal Transformation

We are culturally conditioned to raise children the hard way: in opposition to human nature. A profound shift in consciousness, perceptions, values, and strategies is required for parenting to be the joyful, easy, creative adventure that nature intended.

This personal transformation is the single greatest benefit of applying the ideas in this book. Not only does it make parenting more fun and successful, it lays a foundation for success in every area of your life.

But transformation doesn't happen overnight. It's the combined effect of many inner changes, all of which take hold gradually and unfold more-or-less together.

The list on the next page provides an overview of the shifts that you will experience. They all have one thing in common: they are aspects of an overall shift *from disempowerment to authentic empowerment.*

Putting the Principles Into Practice

Reading and applying *The Daily Groove* often feels more like a *mindfulness* practice than a parenting method. The most important activity is *centering* — maintaining a state of inner alignment and connection to your Center. When you're centered, your heart is open, you're more creative, and you make parenting choices that are uniquely fitted to your circumstances — choices that *feel* right for you and ultimately benefit your whole family.

Part II of this book is designed to help you apply the principles described in Part I — easily and enjoyably. You will transform your parenting journey from the inside out by exploring and applying one simple concept per day.

For additional resources, tools, tips, inspiration, and support, visit my website: **www.enjoyparenting.com**

ASPECTS OF PERSONAL TRANSFORMATION
(from → to)

Conditionality → Unconditionality
outside-in → inside-out
other-directed → inner-directed
being right → feeling good

Scarcity → Abundance
limitation → possibility
hoarding → sharing
problems → solutions

Competition → Creativity
either/or → both/and
right/wrong → what works
pseudo-power → Authentic Power

Domination → Partnership
power *over* → power *with*
win/lose → win/win
separation → Oneness

Coercion → Attraction
demanding → modeling
authoritarian → authentic
dictatorship → leadership

Needs → Desires
should/have-to → would/want-to
avoiding pain → seeking pleasure
motivation → inspiration

Fear → Love
protecting → trusting
fight or flight → tend and befriend
head → heart

Work → Play
struggling → flowing
destination → journey
there/then → here/now

Resisting → Accepting
controlling → allowing
restriction → freedom
no → yes

Smallness → Bigness
shortsighted → big picture
blame → responsibility
at effect → at Cause

The Daily Groove

The brief, practical, inspirational messages ("grooves") in this section offer a multitude of ways to put the principles in Part I into practice. My goal in writing each one was to make it easy and fun for you to chip away at the old paradigm while you create your new parenting groove.

I recommend keeping the book at your bedside or someplace where you'll notice it and remember to read one of the grooves every day, preferably at the beginning of the day. Most of them take less than two minutes to read, and there are enough of them to keep you inspired for about six months.

The order in which you read the grooves is not important: you can read the book from cover to cover, use it like an "oracle" (hold a question or desire in mind and then open the book at random to receive an answer), or browse the pages until something piques your curiosity.

Additional resources for getting the most out of this book are available for free, online at **www.enjoyparenting.com**.

Finding Your Groove...
One Day at a Time

Watching children grow is one of the pleasures of parenthood. Some days you wake up and your child appears to have grown a few inches overnight!

But these apparent quantum leaps are in fact the culmination of countless tiny changes, each of which seems insignificant by itself.

Your inner growth as a parent is no different. You wake up one day and realize you've found your groove! You're enjoying parenthood most of the time, and your "bad" days are now *better* than your "good" days used to be.

And while you'll certainly have "aha!" moments — your *inner* growth spurts — it's the many, small, day-to-day choices that, over time, transform your path through the wilderness of leading-edge parenting into an easily traveled groove.

Today, set an intention to "improve your groove" in some small way that would be easy and fun for you.

Isn't it nice to know that even if you only get 1% "groovier" every day, you'll be 365% groovier in a year?!

Idealism vs. Perfectionism

You can be an idealistic parent without falling into the trap of perfectionism.

Your parenting ideals give you a focal point, a sense of direction on your journey.

But perfectionism demands the impossible: Get to the destination without taking the journey! ("If you can't do it right, don't do it at all!")

If perfectionism is keeping you from enjoying your idealistic parenting journey — if you feel ashamed whenever you fall short of your ideals — consider this funny–but–true saying:

Anything worth doing
is worth doing poorly at first.

You knew that when you were born. That's why you were filled with joy when you took your first, wobbly steps as a baby.

Today, remember that every worthwhile journey begins with a few wobbly steps. And give yourself permission to enjoy the wobbles!

Merging With Your Child's Flow

A child's flow is a powerful force, like the traffic on a highway.

When you want your child to change to a new flow, such as leaving a playground or getting ready for bed, it helps to "merge" with his or her flow first. You can avoid a "collision" if you slow down and check out your child's "traffic conditions" before attempting to merge. Just wait until you feel an opening, then go.

Once you're *flowing together*, it's a lot easier to shift to a new flow.

એ ભ

But what if it takes too long for an opening?

The answer is somewhat paradoxical: The longer you're *willing* to wait, the shorter your wait will be.

You connect with that willingness when you soften your resistance and make peace with What Is.

If you perceive the traffic as "bad" and tell yourself "I'm *never* going to merge!" then you will be too busy resisting to notice the brief, subtle merging opportunities as they arise.

But if you make peace with things the way they are, it frees up your attention so you can focus on your goal and respond the moment an opportunity arises.

Let Your Love Shine

Love is like the sun: every member of your family can fully receive the warmth of your love without depriving the others.

Only when you position them in front of or behind one another does love seem exclusive — giving to some while casting a shadow on others.

Love shines *through* you rather than *from* you, which means you can never really run out of it. When loving your children, your partner, and yourself, there is no limit on how much Love you can shine.

The more you release thoughts of limitation and practice *knowing* that Love is infinite — even when others are temporarily focused on the shadows — the more you will experience parenthood as a sunny, joyful, empowering journey.

Be Self/Centered

If your child is whining for something you'd rather not give, you might notice a knot in your stomach. That means you're NOT centered. ("Knot-centered"?)

Anything you say or do while you're off center is likely to make things worse. Better to get centered first. Take a deep breath and tell yourself...

"I will take no action until I feel centered."

You may find that no other action is needed.

Why?

Bottom line: Children want centered parents more than the things they whine for.

Growing Down

Phrases like "child's play" and "cry like a baby" and "grow up!" expose an unspoken belief of our culture: children are expected to have fun and express their feelings openly, while grown-ups are expected to accept that life is mostly a grind with little room for authenticity.

Perhaps, then, our desire for our children to be happy and authentic is partly a wish for ourselves. Luckily, *modeling* is the most effective parenting tool, so let's model authenticity and lightness today by "growing down"...

- ◆ Eat spaghetti with your fingers
- ◆ Wear shoes that don't match
- ◆ Wear no shoes at all... in the rain
- ◆ Don't delay gratification
- ◆ Scream when you feel like it
- ◆ Pee in the grass!

No need to worry what other grown-ups might think. Just tell them you're sacrificing your adultness for the good of your children.

Resistance Is Futile

You can't resist something without focusing your attention on it. And according to the Law of Attraction, whatever you focus on *expands* in your experience.

So the way to end the unwanted behavior of a child (without resorting to violence) is to *stop trying to end it!*

Instead, look for ways to think differently about the behavior, until you feel your resistance softening.

You might think, "I can understand how he feels," or "She's finding her way," or "It's not the end of the world," or even, "It's *okay* for me to resist this... but I feel better when I let it go."

The less you resist, the more creative you can be, and the more you can *inspire* a change rather than having to force one.

Be Selective... Go Shopping!

Naturally, you want your child(ren) to have experiences that are uplifting and joyful, so you are *selective* about what you expose them to.

But what about YOU? Are you selective when it comes to the things you give your attention to?

Contrary to our nature, our culture trains us to pay attention to things that upset us (like the evening news!) and we forget that we can be selective.

Being selective means noticing how you *feel* as you focus on something and, if it feels bad, changing the channel, so to speak.

It's sort of like shopping for clothes. "Will I feel good in this?" If not, it goes back on the rack and you look for something better.

So, today, notice what you're thinking about your child, and be selective: go "shopping" for thoughts that feel good when you "wear" them.

Go With the Flow...
Even If It's 'Wrong'

Sometimes we think we're doing our kids a favor
when we tell them the "right" way to do something:
"No, dear... Do it *this* way."

We think we're just saving them the hassle of
reinventing the wheel, or preventing something from
being "wasted," or saving time. But our corrections also
send unintended, unspoken messages, like...

- ◆ The end result is more important than the process.
- ◆ Efficiency is more important than joy.
- ◆ There is no value in making mistakes.
- ◆ Better to go with a "sure thing" than to take risks.

In other words, frequently correcting children undermines their (and our) creativity!

So next time you see your child doing something the
"wrong" way, ask yourself if it's really so bad that you
can't go along with it. See if you can relax and enjoy
witnessing his or her process of discovery.

Children who are allowed to find their own way learn
that they *can* find their own way.

Helping vs. Co-creation

Q: How do you know when it's appropriate to offer your child help/assistance?

A: When the offer feels *inspired* rather than fear-based.

If you're coming from a perspective that your child is helpless, damaged, weak, incompetent, lost, wrong, etc., then your "help" will only give power to that belief. It won't feel inspired to you, and it won't inspire your child to connect with his or her Power.

But if you consciously shift your perspective to one in which you see your child as capable of finding his or her way, you won't feel like you "should" help, and you probably won't offer to help unless asked.

However, you might be *inspired* to get involved in a way that doesn't feel like you're a "have" helping a "have-not" — it'll feel more like two souls playing together, co-creating purely for the joy of it!

Have a NICE day!

Most of us have been thoroughly trained to be "nice."
The 2-part **Rule of Nice** goes like this...

Part 1: Only say and do things that please others.

Part 2: If you feel like saying or doing something
that might possibly displease someone,
see Part 1.

So, to obey the Rule of Nice at all times, you have to get
pretty good at *not* being authentic. But being
inauthentic is not very nice, so the only way to win this
game is not to play it!

Children are naturally authentic, which means they
often aren't "nice." You're supposed to pressure them
to obey the Rule of Nice, but wouldn't it be nicer to let
them inspire *you* to be more authentic?

Authentic children, knowing their inherent worthiness,
shamelessly ask for everything they want. Parents
who've bought into the Rule of Nice feel obliged to
fulfill their children's wishes and eventually feel
overwhelmed.

At this point, many "nice" parents snap and become
mean... followed by guilt... leading to more false
niceness. And the nice-mean-guilty cycle repeats.

$\longrightarrow$

Some parents find relief by persuading their children to want less. This seems benign but the end result is the children believing there is something wrong with them: "I want something... but I shouldn't want it... I must be unworthy."

Lasting relief for everyone begins with quitting the niceness game. When you don't "have to" be nice, you may discover that you *want* to be nice!

Even if you choose not to "give in," you can stand in a place of *knowing* that they — and you — are worthy of satisfaction. That's the place where creativity flourishes!

"I'd Rather Feel Good!"

We've been conditioned by the agents of our culture —
parents, teachers, the media, etc. — to believe that our
success and happiness depend on being "right."

Today, let's question that...

When you argue with your child, you may be "right,"
but do you feel happy?

When you criticize your partner, you may be "right,"
but do you feel love?

When you berate yourself for making a mistake, you
get to be "right" about your wrongness! Are we having
fun yet???

If you feel stress today — even mild tension — ask
yourself if you're trying to be "right" about something,
and consider the potential relief of simply letting it go.

Just breathe... and tell yourself, "I'd rather feel good
than be right!"

Beyond Right and Wrong

Children are born knowing that feeling good is more important than being "right." They know their emotions are their Inner Guidance, and they trust it.

So why do they sometimes rebel and seem to care more about being right? One possibility is that you may be telling them something that contradicts their Inner Guidance.

For example, if you say "It's time to go," while their Inner Guidance tells them to stay, they know you are talking crazy talk!

If you say "You shouldn't touch that," while their instinct is to explore, one of you is lying... and it's not them!

You can end conflict and transcend right/wrong thinking by tuning in to *your* Inner Guidance. Give it some time... The heart is slower than the head, but it's wiser, too.

If you go deep enough, you'll find the place where your Guidance and their Guidance overlap — the *common ground* where everyday miracles are born.

Say Yes FIRST

When your child is doing something that's not to your liking, just saying "no" is likely to lead to a conflict.

Respectful parents offer their children alternatives: "Don't do THAT... Here, do THIS."

But if you lead with a "no," the "yes" may not be heard — the child will be too busy defending against what appears to be an assault on his or her freedom.

So look for ways to say "yes" FIRST — if not literally, then energetically — and don't focus a lot of energy on the "no." Let your child be *attracted* to an acceptable alternative rather than forced.

Now you're working *with* your child's nature!

Mother Nature Always Says YES!

Don't be fooled by the media's portrayal of nature as brutal and savage.

Take a walk today with the intention of seeing Mother Nature's life-positive attitude. Look carefully and you'll see that there's no end to the evidence of Well-Being.

When the dandelion asks, "May I grow?" Mother Nature says, "Yes! Here is a good place for you to grow."

When the bumblebee asks, "May I have more nectar?" Mother Nature says, "Yes! Here is a dandelion who wants to share some with you."

When all the creatures say, "May we live joyfully?" Mother Nature says, "Yes! And you need never fear death, for it is a re-emergence into the pure joy of Spirit."

Mother Nature ALWAYS finds a way to say "yes" — to maximize the pleasure of being alive.

As her children, we have that same capacity to say "yes" to pleasure, "yes" to creativity, and "yes" to living joyfully with our own children.

Invisible Teaching

The problem with teaching children *explicitly* is that we are rarely aware of what we are teaching them *implicitly*.

For example, if you tell your children to say "thank you," the implicit lesson is that expressing gratitude is something they *should* do whether they feel like it or not — not something that comes naturally.

Better to say "thank you" yourself — to model the appropriate behavior *joyfully*. Joy is attractive and, eventually, they'll want in on the fun!

Your child doesn't internalize what you *say* as much as the *energy* with which you say it. Pay close attention to how you feel and you'll notice that teaching often carries a subtle vibe that feels "yucky."

So when you must teach explicitly, clean up your energy first. Otherwise you might be teaching the wrong lesson!

When you teach by example, you are following the advice of Gandhi, who said, "you must BE the change you wish to see..."

"What Happened?!"

A crying child runs into the house from outside, seeking comfort. The well-meaning parent's first words: "What happened?!"

This common reaction is one of many subtle ways we teach our children values that we ourselves never consciously chose...

◆ What happened (the past) is more important than what's happening now (the present).

◆ Reason is more important than emotions. You can't simply have a feeling; you have to explain *why*.

◆ Things happen TO you. You don't create your own experience.

A few decades later, this child will be reading *The Daily Groove*, trying to remember to stay *present*, that feelings *are* important, and that we *do* create our own experiences!

The next time you're about to ask your child what happened, decide instead to be still — to be fully present with your child, appreciate his or her emotional journey, and enjoy the feeling of connection.

Your Emotional Guidance

Nature designed our bodies to feel *pleasure* when we do things that are good for us and *pain* when we do things that aren't. For example, eating feels good when you're hungry, but it hurts when you're full.

Just as physical feelings are meant to guide us toward physical well-being, **emotions** are a higher order of feelings meant to guide us toward *spiritual* well-being — that is, to guide our thoughts.

When your thoughts are aligned with your Higher Self, you feel pleasureful emotions like peace and love. When your thoughts are out of alignment with your Higher Self, you feel painful emotions like fear and resentment.

Today, be mindful of your emotions and notice the thoughts that accompany them.

Remind yourself that ALL emotions are good — even the "negative" ones. They are there to guide you back to your Self.

An Example

A mother sees her toddler snatch a toy from his baby sister, who starts crying. The mother is outraged.

The conventional view is that the child's behavior *made* the mother angry. But the cause of her outrage

→

was actually her *thoughts about* the behavior. Those
thoughts flashed by so quickly she didn't notice them.
Thoughts like...

- He's traumatizing the baby!
- What have I done wrong to create that behavior?
- What would my friends think if they saw that?
- I am powerless to stop the behavior without
  resorting to punishments.

These thoughts are out of accord with her Higher Self
who *knows* her limitless creativity and freedom, her
absolute worthiness, and her children's inevitable well-
being.

The anger is her Emotional Guidance telling her she's
gone off track. She will find relief (and eventually her
"groove") by deliberately reaching for *soothing*
thoughts, like...

- The baby always recovers quickly.
- My desire to be a good parent is stronger than ever.
- Whoever judges me is not my friend anyway.
- I can connect with my Authentic Power regardless
  of his behavior.

When she feels relief, that's her Emotional Guidance*
letting her know she's moving her thoughts in the right
direction.

Try it!

---

* The terms *Emotional Guidance* and *Inner Guidance* are used
  interchangeably throughout this book.

Be Unreasonable

When parenting becomes stressful, notice what you're thinking. You'll discover that you have a "good reason" for your stress:

- ◆ I'm worried *because* _____.

- ◆ I'm angry *because* _____.

- ◆ I feel guilty *because* _____.

When you have a good reason to be stressed, the fastest way to release the stress is to let yourself be UNreasonable.

Why? Because it's more important to feel good than to be "right."

Why? Because good feelings are your Emotional Guidance telling you you're aligning with your Authentic Self.

So being unreasonable is actually quite reasonable!

Does this mean ignoring things that need attention? Not at all. It just means you've realized that there is *no* reason good enough to justify sacrificing your peace.

Your connection to Well-Being is always more important.

Boycott That Thought!

Conscientious parents often boycott companies whose products and practices undermine children's well-being. Today, let's play with the idea of boycotting *thoughts* that undermine your parenting vision.

The human mind is like a marketplace of thoughts, and *attention* is the currency with which you "buy into" a thought... or not. You boycott a thought by paying no attention to it — by focusing on a better, more empowering thought instead.

A conventional boycott is only effective if large numbers of consumers participate. But there's only ONE consumer in your thought market: *you*. So when you boycott a thought, that thought's "market share" goes to 0% and it goes "out of business."

When you feel bad about your parenting or your child, it means you're buying into some negative thought or perspective. For example, a thought like "I'm a terrible parent" closes your heart and undermines your creativity, so...

BOYCOTT THAT THOUGHT!

...and give your attention to encouraging thoughts like "I don't have to be perfect... My parenting is gradually improving... I'm finding my way."

"What's GOOD about that?"

If it's raining, you're supposed to call it "bad weather" and complain.

Complaining makes you feel bad, but you've been led to believe that the source of your angst is the rain — the weather *conditions*. That's *conditionality*.

UNconditionality means wanting so much to feel good that you stop using conditions to justify feeling bad.

One way to practice the Art of Unconditionality* in the face of "bad" conditions is to ask yourself, "What's GOOD about that?"

What's GOOD about the rain? It vitalizes the soil and plants... It makes the air smell clean... It's fun to get drenched and then go take a hot bath!

What's GOOD about children "misbehaving"? It means they're trying to engage, explore, connect, create, etc... It means you get to practice loving and feeling good unconditionally, which is the key to your Authentic Power.

Eventually you'll realize it's neither good nor bad — it just IS.

Welcome to Reality!

* See page 211.

Unconditionality vs. Desires

Q: How do you reconcile "unconditionality" with having preferences and desires? If you're totally unconditional, shouldn't everything be fine the way it is?

A: Unconditionality doesn't mean having no preferences or desires; it means that you don't let the temporary absence of your preferred conditions prevent you from enjoying the present moment...

> "When conditions are to my liking, I feel great! (Obviously.) And when conditions are not to my liking, I enjoy anticipating the unfolding of my preferred conditions."

The idea that you can't enjoy this moment because of unwanted conditions is a LIE perpetuated by our conditional culture — a lie that serves no purpose other than to keep people feeling powerless!

Unconditionality says, "Enjoying the here and now is my top priority, so I'm not going to use these conditions as an excuse to separate from my natural state of well-being."

So when your child "misbehaves," or your partner is unsupportive, or you're sleep-deprived, etc., use those unwanted conditions to help you clarify what you *do* want. Then practice unconditionality by accepting the present conditions AND joyfully anticipating the fulfillment of your desires.

Inner Freedom Feels Good

Remember how you felt on the last day of school before the summer break? Even if you *liked* school, you derived pleasure from the sudden expansion of personal freedom, didn't you?

Inner freedom feels like that, too. And you don't have to wait until summer; it's only a thought away!

Today, try playing this game: Every time your child says or does anything, (1) notice your first thought about it, (2) think of some alternative thoughts, and (3) *feel* your freedom to choose.

For example, your child dumps a big box of toys and your first thought is, "Ugh! Another mess for me to clean up!" What other thoughts are possible?

- ◆ I love my child's enthusiasm!
- ◆ I HATE those damn toys!
- ◆ I wonder what s/he's looking for.

Now notice that having a choice feels better than having no choice. The point of the game is not to choose (yet), but to enjoy knowing you CAN choose what to think about any situation.

Doesn't freedom feel good?!

Who's Demanding?

When you feel bothered or overwhelmed because your child seems to be demanding too much, ask yourself, "Who's demanding this of me?"

There's a good chance that a big part of the demand on you is coming from YOU in the form of a "should." If you believe you "should" do something, you are making a demand on *yourself!*

Remember today that you are *free to choose.*

Whatever the request, you don't *have to* fulfill it. When you remember your freedom, your child's demands will feel a lot less demanding.

℅ ℃

Q: What about babies? Don't we <u>have to</u> meet their needs?

Actually, no. Even if you think you have no choice, you are in fact *free to choose* whether to nurture your baby.

Many people are afraid of such freedoms because they've been conditioned to believe that humans are not good-natured — that we only do good when we "have to." Of course that's not true.

Once you know you're free *not* to meet your baby's needs, you connect more powerfully with the part of you that *wants* to meet them.

The Joy of Being Known

Think of a beloved friend or family member who knows you so well s/he can practically "read your mind." Someone who knows what pleases you without having to ask.

Doesn't it feel good to be known like that?

Children naturally want to be known by their parents in that way. But parents inadvertently weaken that connection when they constantly ask their kids what they want.

The idea that it's rude *not* to ask comes from our culture of alienation. In cultures of intimacy, to be asked one's preferences is to be treated like a stranger.

Today, whenever you're about to ask your child's preference, first ask yourself if you already know enough to make a choice that will please him or her. If not, go ahead and ask. If so, act without asking.

If your child objects to your decision, simply take in the new "data" and adjust course, this time or the next. Now you know your child a little better.

The Joy of NOT Being Known

While there is great joy in being known, *not* being known can be a good thing, too — it gives you space to re-create yourself every now and then.

A parent's "knowing" can have the unintended effect of suppressing growth and learning: "Don't give my son any broccoli — he hates it!" Who's to say he won't develop a taste for broccoli today?

If you find yourself using a lot of *labels* (e.g., "fussy eater") you definitely "know" too much about your child!

Today, enjoy connecting with what you know about your child, but also be willing to let go of everything you know and allow a new truth to be born.

Your Emotional Guidance will tell you which way to go.

Creator, or Reactor?

An understanding of *power* is needed to become an effective human being. So children are instinctively driven to discover the nature of power, and they look to their parents for clues.

Our children especially notice our *reactions*. When we react to something, that thing appears to have power.

Whether you react positively (like when someone gives you flowers) or negatively (like when you see a big spider in your house), you are teaching your child that those things are powerful.

- ◆ When you worry about a possession, you give it power.

- ◆ When you are offended by certain words, you give them power.

- ◆ When you react to something in the news, you give it power.

- ◆ When you react to your child's behavior, you give it power.

Today, notice your reactions and consider what they might be teaching your child about power.

By being creative rather than reactive, you demonstrate that Authentic Power comes from within.

The Play Ethic

According to the *work ethic* of our culture, happiness comes from hard work and toil. "No pain, no gain."

This contradicts the *play ethic* of nature: maximizing pleasure while avoiding pain. Nature always follows the path of least resistance.

Children naturally express the play ethic, and a lot of parent-child conflict reflects the clash between the two value systems.

Joyful parenting begins the moment you abandon the work ethic and start taking play seriously. That doesn't mean never working; play is anything done in joy — including "work"!

So if parenting feels like hard work to you, set your sights on a new career of full-time play. But don't change your routine yet. Start with a change in attitude.

Focus on the pleasure potential in every moment and, gradually, a joyful new routine will evolve to match your intentions.

Say YES to Desire

When your child asks for something you don't want to provide, you might fall into the trap of competitive thinking:

"If I say yes, I lose; but if I say no, he'll cry. I lose either way."

Today, try this alternative to competition: The moment your child asks for something, say YES without even thinking. But you're not saying, "Yes, I will make it happen," you're saying yes to the deliciousness of desire and appreciating the unlimited number of ways any desire can be fulfilled.

If the request is specifically for YOU to do it, connect with the broader, underlying desire. For example, if she asked you to play with her, perhaps *any* playmate would do, or maybe she wants to connect with you through *any* activity.

But don't try to solve it. Your "YES-energy" will *attract* an inspired solution. It'll feel like a miracle... but only because it is!

What Is "YES-Energy"?

The next time your child makes a request that you'd normally say YES to, intentionally answer YES with heightened enthusiasm and joy. As you do this, *feel* the extreme "yesness" of your response...

That's "YES-energy"!

YES-energy can also be expressed as optimism, clarity, certainty, peace, alignment, flow, presence, etc. — with or without a *literal* YES. It'll soothe (and often satisfy) your child when a literal YES isn't practical.

You can't "spoil" a child with too much YES-energy. The way to spoil children is to give them too many literal YES's that are *devoid* of YES-energy, such as when parents are self-sacrificing or afraid of how their children will react to a NO.

Today, set the intention to amplify your YES-energy every time you respond to your child — *regardless* of whether your literal answer is YES or NO. This is one of the best ways for you and your child to establish a pleasurable, cooperative "groove."

Red Light, Green Light

Virtually all of us "lose it" with our kids at some point. Then later we say, "I didn't want to yell at my child, but I couldn't stop myself."

If you want to avoid these parent-child "collisions," you have to pay more attention to your "inner stoplight": stress.

Suppose you're worried about getting your child to an appointment on time. Worrying is stressful, so it's a *red light* telling you to stop and get centered before moving on. But long ago you were trained to tolerate stress, so you don't notice the red light. You're on a collision course!

Which parent is more likely to end up yelling, the one who's centered or the one who's stressed?

Today, pay close attention to your subtle feelings. Decide that even "mild" tension or irritation is a red light. Stop, breathe, reach for better-feeling thoughts, and wait for the green-light feeling of *relief* before you take action.

No Regrets

As you progress and become a wiser parent, you may at times feel regret that you didn't "know better" when your children were younger. You may even feel guilty for "damaging" them. If so, let Mother Nature inspire you to a more hopeful perspective.

Have you ever explored a wild forest and appreciated the awesome way in which Life springs forth from the chaos? Then you know Mother Nature never regrets. She learns as she goes and always makes the best of things as they are. She never looks back.

When a tree takes root in the shadows, Mother Nature doesn't regret giving it a "sub-optimum" start in life. She trusts it will bend toward the Light and find a way to thrive. And in doing so, the tree creates its own unique beauty.

She knows that no storm, flood, or fire can stop the endless Flow of Life through her children.

Not Wrong

Here's an experiment you can do today:

Pretend there's no such thing as "wrong."

If your child says or does something you don't like, s/he is not wrong for doing it, nor are you wrong for disliking it.

Even if the behavior is dangerous or violent, your child isn't wrong. And you aren't wrong if you choose to stop the behavior. (Don't try to make logical sense of this, just try it and see what happens.)

Notice how you and your child respond to each other differently when you don't make anyone wrong.

Can you be angry at someone who isn't wrong? And if anger itself isn't wrong, can it be a force for good instead of violence?

When "wrong" is out of the picture, it's easier to follow your heart's desire. You can be real about what you want, and you can allow your child to be real, too.

The Joy of Manipulation

The word *manipulate* means "to handle skillfully." Since the main function of childhood is learning how to handle life skillfully, a "manipulative" child is only doing what comes naturally.

A good relationship is one in which both parties can manipulate each other in ways they both enjoy. They dance with one mind, like Fred Astaire and Ginger Rogers. It's called *attunement*.

When you and your child are well-attuned, the manipulation can be so subtle that all you notice is the pleasure of your connection. But when you're distracted or stressed, your child will escalate to unsubtle, unpleasant cues like crying or whining — whatever it takes to get your attention.

Conventional (adversarial) parenting advice says you mustn't "give in" to such manipulation. The parent "wins" when the child gives up hope.

When you understand that unpleasant manipulation is a symptom of failed attunement, the path becomes clear:

◆ Align with your Self.

◆ Attune with your child.

◆ Focus on the pleasure of connecting.

◆ Everyone wins.

The Big Lie

Do you have "control issues"?

The good news is that being a "controller" is a symptom of being intelligent, creative, and passionate... AND duped into believing the Big Lie of our culture: conditionality.

The Big Lie is that you can't be happy or feel worthy except under the "right" conditions. If you've bought into it, then naturally you will use your personal strengths to try and control those conditions.

For example, if you believe your children have to behave a certain way in order for you to feel good (about them or about yourself), then of course you will try to control their behavior.

Once you realize the purpose of the Big Lie — to control *you* — you'll stop believing it.

Practicing the Art of Unconditionality dissolves the Big Lie (and the "need" to control conditions) by affirming the Ultimate Truth: that you have the power to focus your mind in ways that feel good... under *any* conditions.

Love Train

Imagine you're in a train station awaiting the arrival of a beloved friend or family member whom you haven't seen in years.

You've been anticipating this reunion for days, activating memories of good times you've shared, and you *know* you're going to explode with joy when you finally meet.

The train arrives and people begin deboarding as you balance on your tip-toes, reaching for a glimpse of your cherished guest. You can barely contain the immense love and joy you're feeling. . . .

Now imagine that cherished guest is your child! Not some future adult version but your now/today child, coming off that train, just as eager to connect as you are.

Imagine meeting your child with that same expectation of overflowing love and joy every morning as you rise and every time you reconnect throughout the day.

If you like this idea, imagine it often. Creation begins with imagination.

Acceptance vs. Tolerance

Acceptance is one of your greatest sources of Power. Without it, you couldn't receive or own anything, handle unexpected change, or listen effectively.

In general, acceptance means being at peace with What Is. When you refuse to accept something, you sacrifice your peace.

Non-acceptance creates resistance and shifts your focus away from what you want, toward what you *don't* want.

Can you see, then, how you disempower and undermine *yourself* when you deem your child's behavior "unacceptable"?

But acceptance is not the same as tolerance. It's entirely possible to accept something while choosing not to tolerate it. The difference is how you *feel* in the process.

- ◆ Tolerance *without* acceptance leads to resentment.
- ◆ Tolerance *with* acceptance leads to appreciation.
- ◆ INtolerance *without* acceptance leads to conflict.
- ◆ INtolerance *with* acceptance leads to creativity.

In other words, when you accept (make peace with) What Is — *and* you're clear that you want a change — it's easy to solve (or dissolve) the problem creatively.

Interpret Your Way to Partnership

A babe in arms who "pulls" her mother's hair is only behaving instinctively: all primate infants grasp their mothers' "fur" for stability while their mothers move about.

Tragically, when (human) mothers deem hair-pulling to be inappropriate, hurtful behavior, then something designed by Nature to promote closeness becomes instead a point of contention.

It would be so much easier to go with the flow. Simply leaning into the pull would stop the pain, and the mother could cheerfully redirect the baby's grasp to her clothing, for example.

The key to this shift from painful conflict to joyful partnership — which is possible in any parent-child interaction, at any age — is how you *interpret* your child's behavior. You feel more like a partner when you think, "She's just doing what comes naturally," than when you think, "She's hurting me!"

So today pay close attention to your interpretations, and choose interpretations that feel good and inspire you to acts of partnership.

Rethinking Consistency

Conventional parenting wisdom states that parents
need to "be consistent" in order to maintain their
authority.

Flexible parents — those who are willing to take in new
information and adjust course on the fly — are given
labels like *wishy-washy, spineless, jellyfish, waffling,*
and that shame of shames: *permissive!*

But isn't flexibility a virtuous trait? Isn't flexibility
needed to thrive in the complex, fast-changing world
of the 21st century?

So if somebody suggests that you should be more
"consistent," tell them you *are* being consistent...

- ◆ I'm consistently flexible.
- ◆ I'm consistently following my heart.
- ◆ I'm consistently trusting my instincts.
- ◆ And my love is consistently unconditional.

Riding Coattails

When practicing the Art of Unconditionality, hopeful-
ness and optimism can help you make peace with
unwanted conditions and behavior. You can talk
yourself into a more optimistic groove by "riding the
coattails" of past successes — yours or others'.

Suppose your child is taking a long time to fall asleep,
and you're feeling frustrated. Instead of thinking,
"He's *never* going to fall asleep," which makes you feel
worse, recall past situations that turned out well:
"He *always* falls asleep eventually, and there *have*
been times when he went out like a light bulb."

Then focus on your own experience: "I've handled
challenges like this before... I'm good at waiting when I
relax into it... Some of my most satisfying experiences
involved a lot of waiting, and I've always said it was
worth the wait..." Etc.

A feeling of relief will wash over you as you release
resistance and make peace with What Is.

Paradoxically, outer conditions and behaviors are more
likely to improve once you no longer "need" them to
change.

Protectiveness vs. Trust

Sometimes we think our "job" as parents is to protect our children from ever experiencing pain. Parenting then becomes an endless series of warnings, both subtle and dire.

This approach backfires as it disconnects children from their *inner* Guidance.

When we allow them to risk the pain of skinned knees and bruised egos, they hone their ability to follow their Pleasure. When we don't *impose* guidance on them, they learn to *seek* our guidance when they really need it.

Riding bicycles one day with my daughter, I was about to warn her as she approached a patch of loose gravel, but something in me said, "Button your lip, Daddy!"

My gut told me there was no serious danger, and she stood to gain more whole-body wisdom by *feeling* the looseness of the gravel than by being made to *think* about it.

As your child discovers his or her world, notice when you're about to offer advice, ask yourself whether it's really necessary, and trust *your* Inner Guidance.

The Power of Attraction

Attraction means pulling instead of pushing. The "pull" of attraction is not physical. You attract by focusing your mind. Your thoughts have a sort of "gravity" that pulls matching thoughts, conditions and events into your awareness and experience.

Today, try this experiment...

Think of *one* characteristic that you really, really adore and appreciate about your child. Something that makes you smile when you think about it. Pick a keyword or phrase to remind you of this trait, and write it on the back of your hand. (If your child can read, use a code word or symbol instead.)

The idea is to focus on this aspect of your child as many times as you can today. But don't tell your child specifically what you're doing — the power is in what you think, not what you say.

You might also put little reminder Post-it notes in places like door handles, telephones, the fridge, your car visor — wherever you frequently look or reach.

After a full day of focusing on this aspect of your child, review the day and note how it affected your interactions.

Can you see how, through your intentional focus, you *created* (attracted) that experience?

The Absolute Value of Your Child

If you were forced to study algebra when you were a teenager, it probably didn't occur to you that it would one day come in handy as a metaphor for unconditional love. But here it is...

In mathematics, the "absolute value" of a number is its *magnitude* regardless of whether it's positive or negative. So the numbers +50 and −50 have the same absolute value: 50.

Likewise, practicing the Art of Unconditionality often means disregarding the negative interpretations of a condition or behavior and finding a way to see it in a positive light. For example:

- ◆ Whether your child says "I love you" or "I hate you," you can appreciate the magnitude of her expressiveness and emotional honesty.

- ◆ Whether your child rebels or complies with your wishes, you can appreciate his absolute freedom of choice.

Today as you observe your child, if you see any "negative" behavior then ask yourself, "What is this telling me about the 'absolute value' of my child?"

Transcending Culture

Imagine you're visiting a strange culture where people's perceptions are quite different from what you're used to.

They're offended when you shake their hands, and they're honored when you spit on their feet. They believe that a broken mirror brings good luck, and they compete over who gets the privilege of cleaning the toilets.

After a while, you cease making any assumptions about the goodness or badness, rightness or wrongness of *anything*.

Now you see a little girl start to hit her mother. You await the mother's reaction... Will she be offended? Will she be delighted? Will she be indifferent?

In that moment, you yourself have not assigned any meaning to the hitting. It just *is*.

Congratulations! You've transcended culture and connected with Reality.

As you observe your child's behavior today, pretend you're a stranger in a strange land who doesn't know what s/he is supposed to think about each behavior. Then *choose* an interpretation based on how good you feel when you think that thought.

The Benefit of the Doubt

Have you ever been upset with someone for doing or saying something, only to realize later that you had misunderstood them, and you wished you'd given them "the benefit of the doubt"?

Truth is, everyone deserves that benefit, because ALL upsets are misunderstandings born of conditionality.

And no one deserves that benefit more than children. The younger they are, the more their words and actions are merely "experimental," or rough approximations of things they've observed. They're trying to figure out how life works.

When you give them the benefit of the doubt (for example, by not taking it personally when they experiment with unkind words they've heard others use), children learn that their relationship with you is a safe place in which to grow.

And you benefit yourself, too, because you're doubting your "reason" for being upset. With no such reason, you're left with the simple pleasures of inner peace, heartfelt connection, and appreciation of Life's endless unfolding.

Making Peace With What Is

Once you realize that resisting your child's unwanted behavior actually creates more of it, you may find yourself trying NOT to resist it. But that's just resisting *resistance*, which is more of the same!

Releasing resistance begins with the paradoxical act of *accepting* your resistance, and then accepting the unwanted behavior itself. In other words, making peace with What Is.

The old habit of conditional/competitive thinking might cause you to resist making peace with What Is because it confuses surrender with defeat. But surrendering to What Is, is actually the *victory* of Love over fear. And it's the key to manifesting what you DO want without resorting to violence.

Today, pay close attention to how you feel in your body. Resistance is easy to identify: it always feels tense in some way. When you notice resistance, take a deep breath and gently remind yourself, "I could choose peace instead of this."

Then let Peace choose *you*.

The Power of an Open Heart

Think of something that always opens your heart. It can be anything: an uplifting story or movie, an inspiring song or poem, a glorious sunset, a majestic forest, a beloved friend's embrace, a purring kitten... You get the idea.

Now contemplate it vividly until you actually *feel* your heart opening. Pay close attention to that expansive feeling in your chest, and try to "memorize" it. (For some, the feeling may be quite subtle at first.)

Repeat this process until you can easily recall the feeling of your heart being wide open.

Next, set the intention that — for one full day — you'll deliberately reach for that open-heart feeling *before* you do or say anything to your child... every time.

This is not about being "nice." When you want to say "no," say it with your heart wide open and it'll feel like a yes!

Let go of all preconceived ideas of what an open heart is. Remember it's the *feeling* you're reaching for.

The Now Game

Here's a game you can play to lift your child's spirits. It works especially well for 2- to 6-year-olds but can be adapted for any age.

Sadness, disappointment, worry, guilt, and fear are characterized by a focus on the past or future. Getting focused on the *present* can bring instant relief and is the object of this game.

All players must play by *choice*, so it starts with a gentle invitation or suggestion: "Let's play the Now Game."

It's more effective if YOU play, too. And to be truly present yourself, you must let go of any attachment to the outcome.

The game is simple: Take turns using your *senses* to describe things in your environment until you both feel more present. Use simple "NOW statements" and avoid value judgments. For example:

- NOW I see a blue hat.
- NOW I see the sky.
- NOW I feel the dog's fur.
- NOW I hear a flock of birds.
- NOW I smell a rose.

. . . NOW I feel better!

"Because" vs. "Be Cause"

Today, look out for the word "because" in your prose. Notice that the word is almost always followed by an explanation, justification or reason that subtly assigns power to some external condition.

For example, suppose you decide to leave the park and your child asks, "Why do we have to go?" If you answer, "Because it's time to get ready for dinner," then you're essentially saying that the event called dinner (or time itself) somehow has power over your lives.

A truer, more empowering response would be, "We don't 'have to' go... I'm *choosing* to go." In other words, *you* are the cause... not the clock.

Parents unconsciously avoid such empowering statements for fear that it will lead to a power *struggle*. But you have a choice about that, too. You can choose to express power *with* (rather than *over*) your child.

With a little creativity, you can "be Cause" together.

"Because I Said So!"

You know the scene...

CHILD: Why do I have to?
PARENT: Because I said so!

If your parents ever pulled that one on you, you probably vowed you'd never say it to *your* future kids.

But even the most repugnant acts of unkindness are rooted in life-positive impulses that have been distorted in some way, and there's value in finding the good in such acts.

The good thing about "because I said so" is that it puts your personal power where it should be: in *you*. (And if you *are* pulling rank, it's more honest to say so than to pretend you have no choice.)

Of course, there are many better ways to respond to your child than to say, "because I said so." But you might try saying it silently to yourself every now and then — just to remind yourself that your Authentic Power is within, and it's bigger than all the explanations and justifications you could ever come up with.

Transforming Anger

Amongst peace-loving folks, anger gets a bad rap. This is because anger is usually present when violence is committed.

But anger is a form of *energy* that can be applied constructively, too. That was Nature's intent.

Anger arises naturally whenever you perceive a loss of personal freedom or power. It's there to energize you on your way back to your natural state of empowerment.

If you get angry about some behavior of your child, and then you scold, punish, or yell at him or her, you're simply misdirecting the anger energy.

Just remember: the anger is there to uplift you, not to put down your child (or yourself). It's there to help you break free from disempowering thoughts and reconnect with your Authentic Power.

ℰ ℭ

The transformation of anger begins with acceptance. When you resist anger, it persists, escalates into rage, or descends into depression.

Accepting anger doesn't mean tolerating violence. The compulsion to express anger violently is a byproduct of our *dominator* culture in which *force* is confused with Authentic Power.

→

That compulsion can be greatly reduced if you dis-identify with your anger, which you can do by observing or "witnessing" it.

Take a deep breath and locate the sensation of anger in your body. Use your intuition to sense its subtle qualities. Can you feel its "edges"? What is its "shape," "color," "temperature," "weight," etc.?

Put aside all thoughts of right and wrong for now. Just observe the physical sensation and *be present* with it.

You are not the anger. You are the Witness, observing the anger. Let yourself be curious and eager to discover what anger can reveal. It wants you to remember Who You Really Are.

ℰꙮ ℭℨ

Once you make peace with your anger, you can harness its energy and use it creatively.

Remember, anger always arises from a *perception* of disempowerment. This must be a *mis*perception because Who You Really Are is truly powerful!

So, to reconnect with your Authentic Power, the trick is to **direct the anger at the misperception**. Let yourself get really pissed off that this *lie* has found its way into your mind! It's a rude, obnoxious, uninvited guest!

Once you're consciously directing the energy, you complete the transformation by shifting your thoughts from being angry at the misperception to being *determined* to perceive the higher Truth.

→

If you could put words to this emotionally charged thought-flow, it might go something like this:

> "Dammit! I'm sick and tired of believing that a child's behavior can shut down my heart! My heart and the Infinite Love that fills it are so HUGE that *nothing* can stop them! Nothing but my limiting beliefs, that is, but I'm NOT BUYING IT anymore! I *AM* powerful!! I *CAN* choose what I focus on!! And *I AM DETERMINED* to choose thoughts that *open* my heart!!!"

At this point in your thought process, you can really have some FUN with your aligned anger energy! For example:

> "This is all bullshit anyway, because I *know* deep down that my kid is doing the best s/he can with what s/he's got, and the real reason I'm mad is 'cuz I'm imagining how my parents would react to that behavior... Like it's any of their *freakin'* business!! I don't give a *RIP* what my parents, or the neighbors, or 'society' thinks about my choices! *I AM FREE TO BE THE KIND OF PARENT I WANT TO BE!!!"*

Of course your thought process will vary depending on the situation. The overall strategy is to transform your anger into a *passionate determination* to connect with your Inner Power and Freedom.

Authentic empowerment *feels WAY better* than the shallow satisfaction of forced compliance. And once your heart is open again, all sorts of creative solutions will come flooding in!

The Freedom Paradox

The Law of Attraction is such that whatever you give your attention to — positively or negatively — expands in your experience.

When you *resist* something you don't want, you're giving your attention to it, thus creating more of it.

For example, telling your child "This is a really important phone call, so DON'T interrupt me..." guarantees that you'll experience an interruption — if not by the child then by your own worrisome thoughts.

The key to creating more of what you DO want is to decide that you're free NOT to have it!

When you feel free either way, there's no resistance, which means you can focus on your desired experience.

Today, whenever you notice even a little tension about something, remind yourself of your inherent freedom. ("I'm free to be interrupted, or not.") Then gently shift your focus to your desire. ("I'm going to enjoy this call!")

Balance vs. Bigness

The competitive mindset of our culture leads many parents to put their individual desires and needs first — to the *exclusion* of their children's desires and needs. Others go to the opposite extreme of putting their children first while sacrificing themselves.

Both extremes are unhealthy, so the majority of parents try to find a *balance*. Each party makes some sacrifices so that everyone can get some of what they want.

But you're idealistic and don't want to compromise when it comes to nurturing your children! Fortunately, there's another choice: *expansion*, or as I like to say, "getting bigger."

Smallness says, "My kids won't let me pursue my interests; they want ALL my attention."

Bigness says, "There must be a way we can all be satisfied; I just don't see it yet."

Being open to yet unseen possibilities is what allows you to expand. The question is: *Are you willing to let yourself be as big as you really are?*

The Wild Child

Domesticated animals confined to farms, zoos, and similar unnatural habitats lack a certain "spark" found in their wild counterparts. They've been bred or trained to live apart from their nature. They've adjusted to their lack of freedom.

Put a wild animal in a cage for the first time and behold the fury! What else would you expect from a creature who still knows it's supposed to be free?

Children are born free and wild, and they don't readily submit to "domestication." And thank Goodness for that! Because those who retain that spark are the ones who will uplift the next generation of humanity.

Today, look for evidence of the spark of wildness in your child... and *celebrate* it! Trust that s/he will civilize in due time. And in the meantime, let that spark ignite the flames of an authentic, passionate life.

The Power of Silence

Wordless silence is an invitation to *direct experience.* Unmediated by words. Unfolding in the eternal Now. It's the preferred language of the newborn, and since you were once a newborn, you know it — even if you forgot.

In silence, you can feel your Emotional Guidance more clearly. You can hear your thoughts, and choose them more deliberately. Ten seconds of silence can transform a conversation!

Today, as you interact with your children and others, see how long you can go without speaking. Make a game of it...

- ◆ Talk less but *communicate more* — non-verbally and intuitively.

- ◆ Use body language and touch instead of words.

- ◆ When you have a question, try to "tune in" to the answer instead of asking for it.

- ◆ If the phone rings while you're "in the zone," ignore it.

- ◆ Mouth: closed. Heart: open.

The object of this game is to have fun discovering how much communication is possible without words — to *feel* the qualities of Presence and Connection beyond words.

An Unconditional Icebreaker

Here's a game you can play the next time you're bothered about some unwanted behavior or conditions, especially if you're just beginning to practice the Art of Unconditionality...

First, step back for a minute or so and imagine having the conditions exactly as you desire. Imagine it vividly enough that you activate the *feeling* of having the desired conditions.

For example, say you're annoyed because your child made a huge mess in the house, and you don't want to clean it up. So you close your eyes and imagine the house in perfect order. You might even amplify the feeling by imagining that someone *else* did the cleaning for you — maybe even your child!

Feeling better? Great! Even if you go back to feeling annoyed the moment you open your eyes, you've proven that you don't need the outer conditions to change in order to feel better. How you feel depends only on how you focus your thoughts.

Imagine that!

Weird Is Good!

Our culture is full of contradictions. For example, it's good to be unique and original, but it's not good to go too far off the beaten path... "Don't be *weird!*"

But aren't uniqueness and originality weird by definition?

So let's settle this once and for all: It's *good* to be weird! In fact, the words *weird* and *worthy* have the same root. (Really!)

If you like this book, you're probably a weird parent. You don't *do* conventional parenting, and you probably get strange looks from parents who do. If *you* think *they* think you're weird, it's because they do!

But only because YOU ARE!

So get a piece of paper and write "Weird Things I Do" along the top, then make a list... a LONG list.

When you're done, cross out "Weird Things I Do" and change it to "Things I Appreciate About Myself!"

Now, whenever someone points out your weirdness, you can proudly agree and accept the compliment:

"Thanks!"

Easing Exhaustion from Within

Resistance is holding onto thoughts that block your experience of Well-Being. Worry, frustration, resentment, annoyance, etc. — all are manifestations of resistance.

Clinging to resistant thoughts takes a lot of energy — energy that *could* be easing your path.

Ironically, parents often complain about (i.e., resist) not getting enough sleep. When you resist that condition, the resistance drains your energy, causing you to need even more sleep!

Of course it's good to get as much rest as you can when you're exhausted. But you can also balance the equation from the *inside* by releasing the resistance that creates the stress that makes you tired — including your resistance to tiredness itself.

Today (and tonight) notice how you talk and think about sleep and rest. Gently release any thought that feels stressful. Imagine that every time you release a resistant thought, it's like giving yourself an hour of sleep.

"Do-Over!"

Children in their natural state are totally focused on pleasure. They aim to maximize the FUN in every moment. We can learn a lot about practical happiness by observing them.

For example, when kids are playing a ball game, and the ball lands too close to the line to tell if it's "in" or "out," they don't waste their time and energy arguing about it. There's no fun in that!

Instead, someone calls out, "Do-over!" and they all return to the beginning of the last play to have another go at it.

The do-over is a great tool for parents, too. When an interaction between you and your child turns sour, just stop, remember that you'd rather feel good than be 'right,' and say, "Let's have a do-over!"

Then you can redo the interaction with a clear intention to enjoy it.

My wife and I use do-overs with each other, too. It's way more fun than fighting!

Going Along for the Ride

Here's something you can try if your child enjoys riding "piggyback"...

When you're both in a good mood, offer your child a piggyback ride. But don't lift him/her up; instead, kneel down and let your child *climb* onto your back.

Also, don't try to "entertain" your child (i.e., pretending to be a horse, etc.). Just walk from point A to point B and let the ride itself be the entertainment.

After doing this a few times, your child will begin to recognize your "piggyback mounting position" as an invitation for a ride.

Now you have a "tool" that's especially good for helping your child shift from one flow to another. Instead of saying, "Stop playing; it's time to go," you won't have to say anything — just assume the inviting position and your little rider will eagerly come on board!

Love the Behavior, Too

When a child's behavior is deemed inappropriate, the conventional wisdom is to "Love the child, hate the behavior."

Hmmm… It'd be nice if children could make the subtle distinction between self and behavior, but even adults have a hard time with that! If your partner tells you s/he hates your behavior, is it any less discouraging to hear, "but I love YOU"?

Our behavior is a reflection of who we are at the moment. Hating your child's behavior is like saying you don't love the part of your child that wants to behave that way. To love unconditionally, you must find a way to love the behavior, too.

Fortunately, *loving* unwanted behavior doesn't mean *wanting* it or even tolerating it. You can love unwanted behavior even as you take steps to change it!

But be open to the possibility that Love will transform you, your child, and your relationship, such that you no longer feel a need to change anything.

Don't Explain

Being on the leading edge of parenting, you may find yourself explaining to others *why* you parent the way you do.

This can be a good thing when someone has expressed curiosity about it and you're simply sharing information. But it's better *not* to explain yourself if you're trying to *justify* your choices.

Justifying gives away your power. It implies that you need the other person's approval. It undermines your self-confidence and distances you from your Inner Guidance.

The "need" to explain and justify your choices is based on the "need" to be right. But if your parenting choices are "right," and the other person would parent differently, then s/he must be "wrong." Once you get in that right/wrong mode, conflict or interpersonal tension is inevitable.

Instead of explaining your parenting to others, silently remind *yourself* that your choices are right *for you*, and your own approval is all you need.

Rich With Desire

It feels good to be a "yes-oriented" parent, but how do you respond to your children when they ask for more than you can give?

The real problem is that we've come to believe (and society reinforces the belief) that *we* are the only avenue through which our kids can fulfill their desires.

To find relief from that false burden, you need to start looking for evidence that we live in an abundant Universe which can provide for the fulfillment of all your desires — and your child's.

Then you can celebrate your child's desires without feeling obliged to be the channel through which all of them are realized.

Scenario 1 — Feels Bad

CHILD: I want that bicycle.

MOTHER: (Frowning) I'm sorry, but we can't afford that... Besides, I don't think you're ready... (blah, blah, blah).

CHILD: *Waaaahhhhh!*

Scenario 2 — Feels Better

CHILD: I want that bicycle.

MOTHER: *(Smiling)* Oooh! That's a great bike!

CHILD: Can I have it?

MOTHER: Yes, of course... You can have everything your heart desires... when the time is right.

CHILD: But I want it NOW!

MOTHER: *(Unfazed... smile widens)* Indeed, you do!

CHILD: *(Hopeful)* Will you buy it for me?

MOTHER: *(Checking in with herself... open to the idea... hmm, it doesn't feel right... pleased with her clarity... still smiling)* No.

CHILD: *(Getting frustrated)* But I REALLY want it!!

MOTHER: *(Long pause... gets <u>really</u> centered... waits until heart feels wide open...)* Sweetheart, I know absolutely that you can have this bike or something even better. I also know that you won't be getting it through me, at least not today. But I'm willing to hold this dream with you... I know that if we are clear in our desire and think often about how good it will feel when this dream comes true, it *will* come true. There are many, many ways to receive a bicycle, and Mommy is only one of them. Now, let's take a picture of you sitting on this bike with a big smile, and I'll put the picture on my screensaver so we can rekindle the dream every day when we see it! *(Etc...)*

Of course, this is not a prescription of what to say. It only demonstrates one of many ways a "no" can have a "yes vibe."

Just say yes to your child's authentic desires *and* yes to your own Inner Guidance *and* yes to everyday miracles.

Invisible Abundance

Belief in abundance is crucial to the transformation of your daily *grind* into a joyful *groove*, because virtually all suffering derives from belief in scarcity.

When you believe there is PLENTY of good stuff — time, energy, and especially LOVE — most problems simply dissolve.

For example, you wouldn't worry about your children's behavior if you believed that there's plenty of time for them to find their way, plenty of energy (including money and material goods) to empower them on their paths, and so much love that no amount of "misbehavior" could render them (or you) unlovable.

"But how can I believe in abundance when I see so much physical evidence of scarcity?"

If you paid more attention to your Inner Knowing, you'd "see" much more abundance than your eyes reveal.

Scientists have recently discovered compelling evidence that 95% of all matter and energy is invisible to our physical senses and our finest instruments. That means there's 20 times more "stuff" than we previously "knew" existed!

Today, make a point of noticing whether your thoughts and statements are based on belief in scarcity... or abundance. Which way feels better?

Swashbuckling Through Parenthood

Errol Flynn was an early 20th-century film actor who often played the role of a swashbuckling hero. He truly was a masterful swordsman.

When asked how he handled his sword with such grace, he was known to have said he held it as if he were holding a small bird.

If held too loosely,
it would fly away.

If held too tightly,
it would be crushed to death.

The key to his mastery was staying tuned in enough to *feel* that just-right place between too loose and too tight.

Today, as you interact with your child, pay close attention to your feeling of "holdingness."

Are you holding too loosely?

Open your heart and hold your child closer to its warmth.

Are you holding on too tightly?

Relax your grip and trust that All Is Well.

Needs and Desires

Parents commonly say things like, "You need to put your toys away and get ready for bed."

Such statements put kids in a double bind if they don't *feel* like complying. Who should they believe, their parents or their own feelings? It's a loss either way.

"You NEED to" is really a euphemism for "you HAVE to." It's a way of cloaking coercion.

If you don't intend to give your child a choice, be honest and state your command *as* a command: "Put your toys away and get ready for bed." If that feels rude, maybe your feelings are trying to tell you something!

You may realize that the real issue is *your* needs. That would be a step in the right direction, but don't stop there... A shift in focus from needs to desires is the key that will unlock your creativity.

℘ ℭ

There is no *practical* difference between a need and a desire. For example:

"I need some water."
"I desire some water."

In either case, a drink of water would fulfill the need/desire. The difference is in your perception.

$\rightarrow$

When you're painfully thirsty, your interest in water is perceived as a need. When you feel okay as you are, but would *love* a drink of water, your interest is perceived as a desire.

In other words, needs tend to focus on the painful consequences of non-fulfillment, while desires are more focused on the pleasure of fulfillment.

Our culture takes pain more seriously than pleasure, so we often call our desires "needs" in hopes of having them taken seriously (or to justify forcing the desired outcome).

A more authentic approach is to start taking your desires seriously. That means re-connecting with your inherent *worthiness* — and your child's, too.

Today, notice when you're perceiving your child or yourself to be in need. Acknowledge that the need is valid, but then re-focus on their/your desire and the joyful anticipation of its fulfillment...

Which focus is more inspiring?

Desires Are More Attractive

Understanding that desires are just as valid as needs, and looking for desires where you once saw *only* needs, makes it easier to practice the Art of Unconditionality.

That's because we tend to perceive needs as requirements (conditions) for well-being. For example…

A child makes a mess, and her father thinks, "I feel frustrated because I *need* more order in the house." In other words, he believes his well-being depends on the external condition of an orderly house. His desire for order is valid, but his perception of it as a *need* is disempowering.

Unconditionality means allowing yourself to connect with Well-Being under *any* conditions. It harnesses the power of the Law of Attraction, because once you're focused on Well-Being, you attract more of it into your experience.

When you exude the energy of Well-Being as you focus on your desire, that energy is attractive to your child. As s/he aligns with that energy in you, s/he will be more likely to align with your desire as well.

But this is not a quick fix. Subtle energies take time to do their magic. Fortunately, you'll be connected with Well-Being the whole time!

The Power of AND

Today we'll expand our vocabulary with a new verb...

and: *to include that which is normally excluded.*

When you take two things that are supposed to be exclusive, opposed, or incompatible, and put them together anyway, you are *AND-ing*.

Consider this situation with an exhausted parent:

> "I want to take a nap, *but* my child wants me to play with her. One of us has to lose. It's *either* her *or* me."

To AND that situation, try this perspective:

> "I want to take a nap, AND my child wants me to play with her. Both of us can win. *Both* her *and* me."

AND-ing is an act of faith, because initially you don't know *how* both sides will experience a win. But you trust that in a Universe of infinite possibility, there *must* be a way.

AND-ing opens your creative channels and makes you susceptible to inspiration:

> "Let's play a new game! It's called *The Sleeping Giant!*"

Positive Apology

A conventional apology is rooted in the apologizer's fear of unworthiness. Young children, who *know* their inherent worthiness, rarely apologize except under duress or when emulating adults.

A "positive apology" is possible, however. The *thoughts* behind it might go like this:

> "All Is Well with me *and* you. Our well-being and worthiness are certainties. I am aware that some my past actions were out of accord with who and what I know myself to be. And in that awareness, I have more clarity about how I want to interact with you from now on."

In other words, a positive apology is simply an affirmation of Who You Really Are.

No shame. No blame.

Children aren't picky about how they express such thoughts. It could be as simple as a hug or "I love you."

Next time you feel like apologizing to your child, speak as if you were expressing only love and appreciation. Remember, your "vibe" matters more than your words.

Kids Hear Your Vibe, Not Your Words

The younger your child, the more his or her interpretation of your words is based on the emotional energy they carry — your "vibe" — not the words themselves.

So if your child doesn't listen to your reasonable requests, try this: Listen to yourself as if you didn't know the language and couldn't understand the words; all you have to go by is the tone, the body language, the vibe.

Is it joyful, or heavy? Do you sound eager, or burdened? Does it feel confident, or ambivalent? Is your life a groove, or a grind?

If your vibe is heavy, your joy-oriented child will naturally (and wisely!) tune you out.

Try being silent until you feel centered, connected, and in the Flow. When you speak from that place, you'll emanate an attractive vibe and your child will *want* to align with you.

The (Real) Magic Word

Most of us were taught that "the magic word" is *please*. Just say "please" and you'll get what you want. (Maybe.)

We quickly learned that a certain kind of theatrics was required to unleash the word's magic: begging and *pleading*. But pleading always feels disempowering — not very magical.

Fortunately, there's a word with *real* magic: LET'S.

We used it mostly with other kids, since grown-ups didn't really believe in magic. Nobody told us it was a magic word, we just knew intuitively that we could use it to co-create whatever we wanted:

- ◆ Let's play!
- ◆ Let's pretend!
- ◆ Let's go puddle stomping!
- ◆ Let's make a fairy castle!
- ◆ Let's build a tree house!
- ◆ Let's start a band!

The essence of letting is *allowing*, which is the key to creativity. And the apostrophe-*S* stands for "us," so it really is an invitation to co-create.

$\longrightarrow$

It's good to model politeness and use "please" with your kids, but if it turns into pleading, you're modeling disempowerment. Switch to LET'S and you'll model empowerment through partnership...

Before:
"Would you PLEEEEEASE help me clean up this mess!?"

After:
"LET'S clean this up together!"

The 51% Principle

On your parenting journey, remember that 100% perfection is not required for success. In fact, 51% is enough to guarantee *progress.*

And as a leading-edge parent, progress *is* success. There is no final state of perfection; you'll always be progressing.

Just as an election can be won with only 51% of the vote, you've got lots of room for error. So just relax and look for ways to emphasize and focus on what *is* working.

FEEL Your Way to Find Your Way

Once you understand that the primary purpose of your emotions is to guide your thinking, you no longer need to over-rely on cold rationality to make good parenting decisions.

Your decisions can be "emotional" without being irrational. (They may, however, *transcend* conventional rationality.)

The key is to be willing to *wait*. Take no action until your emotions give you the green light, because your culturally pre-programmed answers come up immediately, while your creative process may take more time.

Often a particular choice seems very reasonable, but you feel *something* isn't quite right. Connecting with the feeling and waiting for more clarity will reveal another aspect that, when considered, leads to a better course of action.

If you have a history of indecisiveness, don't go for "perfect" decisions. When your creative process leads to any feeling of *relief*, consider it a green light for a *good enough* decision. You can always amend your decision later.

Implicit Validation

Much is said about the importance of *validating* children's feelings — telling children that it's okay to feel how they feel.

What's rarely acknowledged is that children innately *know* their feelings *are* valid, so they don't need validation unless they've been previously *in*validated.

When the child's inherent sense of worthiness is intact, the real beneficiary of explicit validating is the parent whose feelings were invalidated in childhood.

Children derive greater benefit from *implicit* validation, which is most powerfully expressed when we are willing to be fully present with them as they move through their emotions.

No words are needed to validate implicitly. You never say, "It's okay to be happy," you just *know* it's okay. So why say, "It's okay to be sad/mad/etc," if so-called "negative" emotions are just as valid as the "positive" ones?

You'll find it easier to stay present if you hold this thought: *Children who have strong feelings are blessed with strong Inner Guidance.*

Nothing but Roses

The age-old advice to "stop and smell the roses" is more poignant than ever in these times of over-scheduled, task-driven lifestyles.

As adults, that could mean taking a few minutes a day to appreciate the little things that add sweetness to our lives. But for children, especially the very young, virtually *everything* is a rose!

Imagine stepping outside and witnessing a total eclipse of the sun that reveals a glorious meteor shower, accompanied by a choir of dogs howling in three-part harmony! Everything is *that* extraordinary to younger children because they haven't been around long enough for very many things to seem "ordinary."

So the next time you're in a hurry and your child is "dawdling," remember that s/he is simply smelling the roses.

Let your child inspire you to don your own "beginner's mind" and experience the fresh uniqueness of this "ordinary" moment.

Generalizing Desires

Suppose your child wants to bounce on your friend's antique sofa, but you want to respect your friend's property. The conventional response is to say NO and block the child's behavior, using force if necessary.

Being *un*conventional, you ask yourself instead, "How can we *both* have what we want?" But these specific desires are incompatible. So you *generalize* one or both of them by looking for the *underlying desires*.

For example, your child wants to jump on the sofa because it feels good to defy gravity. You want to respect your friend's property because you want to be a good friend.

Now you can put these more general desires together and begin to see ways they could fit. Perhaps you could be a good friend to your child by helping him or her find another way to defy gravity.

Keep looking deeper and you'll find many, more general desires that will lead you to an abundant supply of mutually satisfying choices.

Be Real

Presumably, you want to be a respectful, creative, loving parent — and you'd rather not *ever* be coercive with your child. Wonderful!

But what about those times when you're just in a bad mood and don't feel like being a super-parent? Must you sacrifice your authenticity, fake a smile, and go through the motions?

You can try, but it won't work. Even if self-sacrifice "works" superficially, it leads to resentment or rage that eventually hurts everyone.

Here's a twofold alternative: First, give yourself permission to be *real*. Stop trying to hide how you really feel. (Kids always know intuitively how their parents feel, anyway.)

Second — and most important — make a solemn commitment to take responsibility for your feelings. In other words, you won't blame your child for how you feel. You won't blame yourself, either, because authentic responsibility has nothing to do with blame.

Breakthroughs happen when you honor your "negative" emotions without making anyone wrong.

There is only YES

According to the Law of Attraction, whatever you give your attention to, you attract more of.

That means there's effectively no such thing as NO... There is only YES!

If you tell your child, "No, you may NOT have any candy! It's BAD for you! You *shouldn't* eat that junk," then you're essentially saying YES to candy by focusing so much attention on it. The more you resist it, the more you're thinking about it, which guarantees more and stronger thoughts about candy (or whatever you're resisting).

The key to happiness in a YES-based universe is to give very little attention to what you *don't* want, and lots of positive attention to what you *do* want.

If you truly believe your child is better off without something, then look for something else to say YES to — preferably something even more attractive.

Remember that Life Energy and Unconditional Love are more attractive than any *thing*.

The Joy of Sharing

Imagine yourself back in the throes of puberty, and you're madly in love with someone who doesn't yet know how you feel...

> *You're at a park, enjoying an ice cream cone, when your would-be lover walks by, sees you, and smiles! You offer your beloved a bite of your ice cream, and you're OVERJOYED when the offer is accepted!*

Back to the present... Now imagine you're eating some delicious strawberries. You only have two left, and you intend to savor *both* of them. Then your child sees the strawberries and says, "I want one!"

Are you as thrilled to share with your child as you would be in the first scenario? If not, why the difference? (Hint: love trumps scarcity.)

The way to raise kids who *enjoy* sharing is for you to enjoy sharing with *them*. Frequently offer them bites of your food, for example, and let them know how good you feel when you're sharing.

When your child doesn't feel like sharing something with a sibling or playmate, rather than forcing them to share (which isn't really sharing), find something that *you* can share joyfully.

As you consistently demonstrate *your* sharing ethic, they will eventually discover the joy of sharing for themselves.

A Human Becoming

In a product-oriented culture, there's a tendency to "productize" and "package" people. We often forget that a human being is a living process — a "human becoming."

Children are especially dynamic — often visibly different from one day to the next — and no two children develop precisely the same way. This can be a challenge for us when we've been conditioned to "need" the predictability (read: controllability) of static products.

Many parent-child struggles can be avoided simply by allowing children to be different than they were the previous day, or even the previous minute! A toddler may "hate" peas at the beginning of the meal and "love" them by the end of the meal, provided the parent doesn't pronounce the child a pea-hater in the interim.

Today, be mindful of the way you talk about your child. Note that *labels* tend to productize. You can avoid labels by focusing on the process. For example, "he's a fussy eater" becomes "he's figuring out his tastes."

Especially avoid "always" and "never" statements like "she *never* brushes her teeth willingly." Someday she will!

Unconditional Presence:
The Oak Tree

Imagine a great Oak Tree. It knows where it stands, and it holds powerfully to its position. But it doesn't *defend* its position — it's simply *there.*

You can drive a car into the massive trunk of the Oak Tree, and the car will be smashed while the tree remains standing. It's not standing *against* you, and it doesn't take your destructive behavior personally. It just remains rooted... focused... present. Unconditionally.

Now imagine that you *are* the Oak Tree... How does it feel to be so powerfully positioned? Isn't it nice to know that no one can uproot you? Would you even bother to resist? Or would you simply relax and enjoy being right where you want to be?

Next time you feel "uprooted" by your child's behavior, emotions, or any other conditions, remember the unconditional presence of the Oak Tree. Stand rooted in the ground of infinite Well-Being.

There is nothing to resist... All is well.

No Consequences

In our culture, everyone is trained to ignore their Emotional Guidance and replace it with arbitrary rules of "right" and "wrong." Here's a thought game you can play to reconnect with your Guidance in parenting situations...

When you're not sure how to respond to a particular behavior of your child — when your mind is flooded with thoughts of what "they" say you "should" do — ask yourself this:

> **"What would I *feel* like doing if I knew there could be no negative consequences?"**

In other words, pretend you have the magical power to guarantee that (a) nothing bad will happen to anyone and (b) no one will disapprove of your actions. You're completely free to do what most pleases YOU.

You may be surprised by what you discover when you allow yourself to be guided entirely from within.

Of course there *are* consequences to every action. The purpose of this game is not to ignore them forever, just long enough to connect with your authentic Inner Guidance.

Why?

The next time some friend or relative warns you that your parenting style is too permissive, do what any self-respecting 3-year-old would do: Ask, "Why?"

"Because children need limits."

"Why?"

Most people who hold this belief have never questioned it. Those who are willing to examine it might notice that life presents children with many, many limits, and maybe they *don't* need their parents to add even more.

But some will answer with yet another unquestioned belief: "Because they need to learn that they can't always get their way."

"Why?"

Be as relentless as a 3-year-old! Now you're getting to the root of the distortion: the *scarcity principle*.

Maybe he or she is ready to entertain the possibility that we live in an abundant universe — that life is not a zero-sum game.

Or maybe he or she will resort to fundamentalist rhetoric: "That's just the way things are."

"Why?"

Emotional Midwifery

Today, if your child behaves in a way that you find particularly annoying or upsetting, try this perspective:

My child's behavior is <u>not</u> what's really upsetting me. The behavior is triggering unresolved feelings that have nothing to do with the present situation.

In other words, your child is doing you a favor! S/he's giving you an opportunity to heal — to resolve an old hurt and release the stress it has been creating.

You don't even have to figure out the cause of the unresolved feeling. Just *allow* yourself to feel it, and it will resolve naturally. The following will help:

- ◆ Take some deep breaths and locate the feeling in your body.

- ◆ Don't judge, express, or react to the feeling; just be present with it, and let yourself experience it, even if it hurts. (Notice it hurts less if you don't resist it.)

- ◆ Be like an empowering midwife to the feeling, which is giving birth to new awareness, clarity, and freedom.

- ◆ Silently bless your child for playing a part in your healing.

Get In a Receiving Mode

Being idealistic parents means we do a lot of asking.

When you're upset by your child's behavior, when you fall short of your own ideals, or when you see other parents mistreating their children, your reaction is a kind of asking. You're asking for a more harmonious, parent-friendly, child-honoring world.

Well, you can ask and ask and ask, but you won't receive much of what you're asking for until you stop asking and get in a *receiving mode*:

1. Let go of the question and assume the answer is already on its way.

2. Enjoy your expectation of satisfaction and silently give thanks in advance.

3. Be willing to wait "forever" for the answer/fulfillment. The longer you're willing to wait, the more quickly it will come.

An Example

Your child has forgotten to flush the toilet for the umpteenth time this week, and you're feeling increasingly frustrated.

Your child can *feel* your expectation of continued frustration. S/he is naturally cooperative and will continue to meet your unspoken expectation until you put yourself in a receiving mode. . . .

1. Assume that what you want is already on its way.

"My child knows what I want, and it's only a matter of time before s/he gets it down. With my emotional cross-currents out of the way, s/he'll easily settle into a new competency that s/he can feel good about..."

2. Enjoy your expectation of satisfaction and silently give thanks in advance.

"I feel good *now* when I imagine my child successfully forming a good habit. The success is not just the outcome but the whole process, which has already begun. I'm grateful that all I have to do is 'find the feeling place' of having what I truly want, and my child will naturally tend to align with it..."

3. Be willing to wait "forever" for the answer/fulfillment.

"I create satisfaction from within, unconditionally, so there's no hurry. I can actually *enjoy* waiting and witnessing the unfolding process. I like the *whole* story, not just the last chapter. The fulfillment is just the icing on the cake!"

Does that mean you'll never again remind your child to flush? No. But if/when you do, it won't feel like nagging or pleading; it'll be an expression of your positive expectation.

Today, practice getting in a receiving mode as you interact with your children, your peers, and society at large. Can you *feel* the difference between asking and receiving?

Hindsight In Foresight

Think of something you *like* about yourself.

No matter how humble you are, you wouldn't be reading *The Daily Groove* if you didn't believe yourself to be *groovy* in some way!

But you weren't always so groovy, right? Before you found that particular groove, you were groove*less*. Your life is a work in progress, and you *are* progressing.

You get a little groovier every time you learn something, and you've learned a LOT from your life experience — including your "failures."

Some of your best qualities were once failings! So why not look ahead to the time when you'll look back on *today's* "failings" and see them as precursors of grooviness?

You can use this "hindsight in foresight" with your kids, too. When they seem to be getting something "wrong," imagine them ten years from now, by which time they'll surely have it down. From there, you can look back on today's mishap and *appreciate* it as a part of their learning process.

Healthy Selfishness

Conventional thinking has it that if children get "too much" of what they want, they'll become narcissistic adults who only care about themselves.

But this thinking is locked inside the box of the *dominator* paradigm, where you "win" by exploiting, excluding, or defeating others. Outside the dominator box is *partnership*.

In partnership it's understood that we're all connected, so *your* wins are *my* wins, and vice versa. Children internalize partnership values when their parents believe that Love is abundant, because such parents tend to nurture generously and unconditionally.

Younger children are naturally narcissistic. When parents model the "healthy selfishness" of partnership and don't resist their children's narcissism, the children will eventually learn that it feels good to care for others.

Today, notice all the ways in which *giving* makes you feel good, and how others feel good when you allow them to give to you. Let the line between giving and receiving dissolve. That's the magic of partnership!

Confidently Uncertain

When parents are confident, centered, and certain, their children tend to feel more secure, relaxed, and cooperative.

But as parents on the leading edge — constantly blazing new trails and facing the unknown — confidence and certainty don't always come easily.

The trick is to practice the paradoxical art of being **confidently uncertain.**

Instead of pretending you know what you're doing (which doesn't work), you enthusiastically *embrace* your cluelessness! Then you focus on your ability to find your way...

> *"I have NO IDEA how to handle this situation! But I know I can figure it out. I've faced the unknown and found my way before, and I can do it again."*

This works for kids because their security is based on feelings rather than logic. They can feel your confident vibe, and that's enough.

Today, make a list of your personal journeys from clueless to competent. Recall these whenever you're uncertain and want to feel confident anyway.

The Shadow of a Doubt

If you're worried about what others think of your parenting, consider this:

MAYBE they're judging you; maybe not. But *you* are DEFINITELY judging yourself!

Your emotional reaction (worry) is the tip-off to your self-judgment. If you were absolutely confident in your parenting, you might be *aware* of others judging you, and that would inform your choices, but it wouldn't get under your skin.

This doesn't mean you should try to eliminate all doubt. Uncertainty is a necessary part of any leading-edge path. It makes you a better learner.

When you embrace doubt and practice being confidently uncertain, you'll stop needing others' approval. Better yet, some of them will drop their judgments and grow to appreciate or even emulate your ways!

For the New Year

Remember Your Purpose

Imagine... A lovely, sunny day. You're alone in a grassy field, kicking a ball around. You have no goal but to enjoy yourself — pure fun!

Some friends show up and join you in play. Someone suggests a game of soccer, so you establish boundaries, goals, and teams. This focuses and intensifies the shared excitement and fun.

Soon, without even noticing, you get so involved in the game that you forget why you were playing in the first place. You become so afraid of losing that the *fun* is lost.

But then you remember, "Oh, yeah... This was supposed to be FUN!" and you're back in your groove, instantly! You feel even more empowered as you realize you transformed the game entirely from within — unconditionally.

Today, let go of any worries that prevent you from being fully present with your kids, and remember that parenthood is supposed to be fun.

That's what Nature intended... And so did you!

For Valentine's Day

The Love Game

Think about how good you feel when someone tells you they love you — *really* love you. Wouldn't you like to feel that way more often?

The object of today's game is to rekindle that feeling *all day long!* Here's how:

> *No matter what your child does or says to you today, <u>interpret</u> every expression as if s/he said "I love you!"*

This may seem frivolous or even crazy, but don't knock it 'til you've tried it!

You can make up reasons if you like. (Example: "My child loves me so much, s/he'll do *anything* to get my attention.") But there's even more power in perceiving love for no reason at all.

Immense power and pleasure are available to you by deliberately choosing interpretations that feel good *to you*. Before long, you may discover more Love than you know how to let in.

Remember that love is your birthright. You don't need an excuse to let it in. Love is always there for you.

Just breathe and let it in!

Every Day Is Mother's Day!

On Mother's Day we honor and appreciate all mothers for the many ways they bless our families. But the holiday is often tainted by our culturally induced tendency to glorify *self-sacrifice.*

When mothers are treated like royalty for one day as a reward for their selfless devotion to the family, it subtly undermines the partnership between mothers and those they care for, *and* it perpetuates the notion that mothering is a grind the other 364 days of the year.

So here's a radical proposition for every mother who has ever bought into the idea of self-sacrifice as a virtue:

Decide that EVERY day is Mother's Day! Don't settle for anything less than a predominantly pleasureful path of mothering.

And remember that the best way to raise kids who enjoy life is to let them see your commitment to enjoying life yourself!

Independence Day for (R)evolutionary Parents

Parents who practice Attachment Parenting are often accused of neglecting their children's development of independence. "You've got to teach them to sleep alone, to soothe themselves," we are warned.

Strangely, these warnings usually come from the same folks who advise us to take swift disciplinary action the moment our children exhibit signs of independence, now re-labeled "disobedience."

Thankfully, we have the reassurance of the Founding Mothers and Fathers of holistic parenting whose "spoiled" kids are growing up to be remarkably independent!

So let's write our own Declaration of Independence from the culture of alienation:

> *We hold these Truths to be self-evident, that all* **Children** *are created* **Lovable**, *that they are endowed, by their Creator, with certain unalienable Rights, that among these are Life, Liberty, and the Happiness of* **Parental Proximity**...

For Halloween

Matters of Life and Death

The cost of resisting death is high — it sucks the life out of you!

Resisting death, either literally or figuratively, is at the root of many if not most parent-child conflicts. One example is when parents spank toddlers to deter them from running into the street.

When parents worry about how much sugar their children will consume on Halloween, they're essentially resisting death. The life-draining, joy-killing effects of worrying may be greater than the damage done by the sugar!

But making friends with death doesn't mean promoting it. Love, unhindered by fear, always leads to more aliveness.

Love of life inspires ideas and actions which promote safety, health, or whatever you desire — without sacrificing the sacred trust between you and your child.

When you embrace death as an aspect of life, and connect with the eternal essence of Life, you can relax and start enjoying the life you have — here and now.

For Election Day

Creative Democracy

An actual conversation with my daughter...

"What's that sign, Daddy?"

"That's a political sign for the upcoming election."

"What's an election?"

I did my best to convey the abstraction of democracy to a 5-year-old. "Do you know what voting is?"

"No."

"Okay... Pretend we're deciding what to make for dinner, and we're choosing between pizza and spaghetti. Each of us gets to vote for which one we want... Which one would *you* vote for?"

"I want pizza AND spaghetti!"

Suddenly *I* was the student, and the lesson was clear: either/or, win/lose thinking is not something our kids are born with. It's learned. Even if we don't actively teach it to them, we teach it passively whenever we take scarcity and competition for granted.

Today, pay close attention to your decision-making processes — your private "elections." Are they based on scarcity and competition, or abundance and creativity?

Are you willing to concede your contentious elections and surrender to the creative process?

A Post-Modern Thanksgiving

Transforming your life experience (including parenting) from a *grind* to a *groove* leads to a peculiar realization: It's all GOOD... even the "bad" stuff!

There are hidden blessings in *every* situation. You may not see some of those blessings for quite some time — perhaps years — but who's to say you can't enjoy them before you know what they are? Don't you enjoy receiving a gift even before you've unwrapped it?

So when you celebrate Thanksgiving, try giving thanks for things that don't normally garner your gratitude:

- Your child's crying, whining, aggression, etc.

- The person who judged or criticized your parenting.

- That thing you said or did to your child that you promised you never would.

Allow yourself to appreciate that LIFE IS GOOD... *all* of it! Acknowledge the gift of *shadows*, without which the Light would have no depth.

Have fun!

Part-Time Santa, Full-Time Visionary

On gift-giving occasions such as Christmas, Hanukkah, and birthdays, parents traditionally take on the role of a "santa" — a saintly giver who fulfills children's material wishes.

But if your child's wishes exceed what you believe you can or should fulfill, you might forget that you are *not* your child's only means of satisfaction. In an abundant Universe, there's an infinite number of ways any desire can be satisfied.

This year, take the perspective that being a santa is just a "part-time hobby," and that your "full-time job" is to HOLD THE VISION of your child eternally connected to Infinite Well-Being.

In that vision, desire is a blessing, not a demand, so you can celebrate your child's desires even when neither of you knows *how* the desires will be fulfilled.

When you *expect* your child's wishes to come true — somehow, someday — and your child can *feel* your faith... there is no greater gift!

Love Notes to Myself

Ever wish you could go back in time and share the wisdom of your experience with your past self?

"If only I knew then what I know now..."

In your imagination, such time travel is possible and can be healing. But you can do it for real in reverse: share your present wisdom with your future self!

Here's how:

1. Write a bunch of short, inspiring "love notes" to yourself on small pieces of paper. Say things like "Love is the answer," "All Is Well," "Truth will set you free," "Let go!" etc.

2. Hide the notes in places where you'll find them unexpectedly in the future — in a cookbook, your car's glove box, a file folder, a coat pocket, etc.

3. As you hide each one, hold the thought that you'll find it at the precise moment when you'll need to remember that bit of wisdom.

Your child(ren) can play this game, too, and you can also write love notes for each other. There's no right or wrong way — just follow your heart.

Feeling Good vs. Being "Right"

Want to have a great day? Simply decide that feeling good is more important than being "right," and let that priority guide every thought, word, and deed throughout the day.

When being "right" is your priority, you may achieve the shallow satisfaction of receiving approval, but it disconnects you from your Inner Guidance, which is revealed through your emotions.

When feeling good is your priority...

- ◆ You choose love, because loving always feels good.
- ◆ You choose connection, because it feels better than separation.
- ◆ You choose forgiveness, because resentment feels yucky!
- ◆ You choose appreciation, because it makes you feel rich!
- ◆ You choose responsibility (not to be confused with blame), because it feels empowering.

See what happens when you take a day off from being "right" or trying to be a "good" parent. Let go of all "shoulds" and let yourself be guided by pleasure instead.

But don't settle for the initial, fleeting pleasure of rebelling against the shoulds. Keep going... Hold out for the deeper pleasure of connecting with your Authentic Self.

Two Kinds of Responsibility

The word *responsibility* can be confusing because its meaning changes depending on the "active worldview" of the person using it.

The old worldview is one of scarcity and competition, where one seeks empowerment through controlling people and conditions, and by being "right." In that worldview, responsibility means obligation, duty, and/or blame.

The new worldview is one of abundance and creativity, where empowerment comes from within and is expressed through partnership. In that worldview, responsibility is the *ability to respond* creatively, and it's an acknowledgment that each individual creates his or her own experience of life.

Today, pay close attention to how you feel when you're trying to be a "responsible" parent. If taking responsibility makes you feel heavy, burdened, guilty, ashamed, or resentful, then it's time to upgrade your worldview!

Relieving Time Pressure

You enjoy parenting most when you feel expansive and flowing — the way you feel when you're not under any kind of pressure.

One of the most common pressures of modern life is *time pressure*: having to be somewhere or do something by a certain time. Young children naturally live in the moment, not by the clock, so subjecting them to time pressure usually leads to discord.

To reduce time pressure in your daily groove...

◆ Decide that geniality (feeling good) is more important than punctuality (being "right").

◆ Don't agree to be on time — build flexibility into your agreements. ("I'll be there around 7:00-ish.")

◆ When you really want to be on time to an appointment, give yourself LOTS of extra cushion time — just accept that life with kids is less "efficient."

◆ Don't rush when you're late — call and renegotiate! For all you know, the person you're meeting may be late, too.

◆ When you can get away with it, don't make plans at all! Enjoy living spontaneously!

From REactive to PROactive

Reactive parenting is like an airplane on auto-pilot flying off-course: to set a new course you must first get control of the plane on its *present* course.

That means, paradoxically, that you can avoid an unwanted reaction by deciding to do it *deliberately!*

Example: You're about to yell at your child, and you can't stop yourself. So you decide to yell *on purpose*, with the full force of your deliberate intention! BUT...

You alter the outburst in some way that makes it benign, like singing a really high/loud note instead of yelling, or changing your words to "Blabbety! Blabbety! BLAH!" Anything that works *with* your emotional energy rather than against it.

Once you've shifted from REactive to PROactive, you can direct your energy *consciously*, in accord with your ideals.

This technique is not a panacea, but it works especially well with *mild* reactiveness — often turning potential conflict into playful fun!

Seeing the Forest for the Trees

If we define "Well-Being" as the free flow of Life Energy, there is ample evidence that our world is a place of breathtakingly abundant Well-Being!

But we perceive a *lack* of Well-Being when we focus narrowly on situations in which that Flow is temporarily blocked — when we focus on "what's wrong." It's like looking at a single diseased tree and forgetting that the forest is alive and well.

When a child cries or indicates distress, most parents automatically ask, "What's wrong?!" The more intensely we ask, the more we lose touch with the abundance of Well-Being in and around us.

Today, if your child is distressed, try letting go of needing to know what's wrong. Remember that simple Presence is the cure-all for most distresses, and connecting with Well-Being makes you positively, powerfully present.

Relax your focus and "zoom out" until the problem looks tiny and Well-Being looks huge. Let yourself see the "problem" as an integral part of the big picture of Well-Being.

Life Is Messy... Get Over It!

In man's quest to conquer nature, our culture has developed an unhealthy aversion to the natural messiness of life.

Heaven forbid you should eat an apple that isn't nice and round and free of bug bites. Those get made into applesauce so we never have to see their messiness!

And if our high-tech, Star Trek fantasies were real, we could avoid the messiness of birth and simply "beam" babies out of the womb — without a drop of blood in sight.

Even if you're a "crunchy" parent who's not afraid of nature's messiness, there may be other kinds of messes you abhor, like the messy ways children learn, explore, and process emotions. Or the messy way *you* grow through parenthood.

Today, whenever you feel bothered about anything, ask yourself, "What 'messiness' am I resisting?" Are you not allowing your *own* process to be messy?

Well, get over it! Life *is* messy.

Let life's messes remind you how good it is to be ALIVE!

What Makes Kids So Wonderful?

Answer: Kids are wonderful because they're
FULL OF WONDER!

They wonder constantly, and wonder leads to exploring which leads to play which leads to creation which leads to more wonder.

Well... If kids can do it, so can you.

You don't have to be a perfect parent to be a *wonderful* parent. You need only to *wonder...*

"I wonder who my child is becoming."

"I wonder why some behaviors bother me so much."

"I wonder what would happen if I ignored all the mind chatter and followed my heart."

"I wonder if I can still do cartwheels."

Your assignment for today: Be wonder–FULL!

WWCD: What Would a Child Do?

A popular Christian slogan is "WWJD: What Would Jesus Do?" This is an excellent question for Christian parents to ask as Jesus honored children, promoted nonviolence, and embodied unconditional love.

Anyone you consider to be loving and wise can help you connect with your Inner Wisdom in this way:

- What would the Dalai Lama do?
- What would my great aunt Sally do?
- What would Mister Rogers do?
- What would my dog do? (Seriously!)

Another great source of wisdom is *children*, who constantly present us with opportunities to let go of limiting beliefs:

- A child would care more about feeling good than being "right."
- A child would look for the FUN in every situation.
- A child would be open to miracles.
- A child would be authentic.

Today, include children's wisdom in your decision-making by asking yourself, "What would a child do?"

Patience vs. Presence

The root of the word *patient* means "to endure." Patience is normally seen as a kind of self-sacrifice in which one tolerates unpleasant conditions for prolonged periods.

When you understand that self-sacrifice ultimately hurts both the self and the intended beneficiary, you have to wonder if patience is really "a virtue."

But what about parents who are truly calm, centered, and creative even when their children "misbehave" — aren't they being patient?

While bystanders may look at them and see patience, the parents themselves aren't experiencing unpleasantness, much less "enduring" it. More likely they're *enjoying* the creative process.

Today, try replacing patience with *presence*. Be willing to be present with What Is, no matter what arises. Return frequently to your heart's desire and let it inspire your actions.

Others will call you patient, but you'll just call it... happy!

PREsponsive Parenting

Raising a child in harmony with human nature is like driving to a distant city. The road isn't straight, but it'll get you there.

For example, the road to independence as an adult is via dependence as a baby. Going straight to independence is a disaster.

You know you've veered off course when the ride becomes suddenly rough, so you steer back to the smooth road. Responsive parenting is like that: answering a baby's cries or a child's aggression with unconditional love and nurturing.

But when driving, you *rarely* veer off the road. You stay *centered* in your lane for a smooth ride! You stay *attuned* to the road, so you can adjust course *before* you veer off.

In other words, you can be **pre**sponsive!

Today, if you hit a rough spot with your child, be *re*sponsive, but also consider how you might have *pre*sponded, and refine your attunement accordingly.

Pleasure-oriented *pre*sponsiveness can turn your parenting journey literally into a JOYride!

WordWatch: Always/Never

Today, notice whenever you use the words **always** and **never**.

The power of these words is in their ability to *finalize* — to make something seem "written in stone" — and to establish a strong *expectation*. For example:

"He **always** throws a tantrum when we leave."

"I **never** get enough sleep."

Remember, you tend to get what you expect, so when you hear yourself say such things, rephrase them using softer words that leave open the possibility of improvement:

"*Sometimes* he throws a tantrum when we leave. (Maybe this time he'll be fine.)"

"It's been a *long time* since I got enough sleep. (Perhaps I can sneak in a catnap today.)"

But *do* use always/never with uplifting thoughts:

"She **always** finds her way."

"I **never** make mistakes that I can't recover from."

Goodness Is Inspired, Not Required

Situation 1:

You ask your friend what she wants for a birthday gift, and she says, "I would treasure *any* gift from you!"

Wouldn't you feel inspired to give her something very special?

Situation 2:

Another friend says, "I hope you're getting me something *good* for my birthday... I just *hate* tacky gifts!"

Wouldn't you feel like giving this friend a pile of fake dog poop?!

The point is that you feel most inspired to please others when you don't feel pressured or coerced — when you don't "have to."

Children are no different. They love to please others, especially their parents, so long as their inspiration to share pleasure isn't confounded by implied threats of punishment, reward, or withdrawal of approval.

Today, let go of all "required goodness" by affirming that your child is inherently good, and is *free* to express that goodness... and free *not* to express it.

Remember that the best way to foster children's authentic goodness is to let them see how much *you* enjoy expressing your own goodness.

"I Didn't Sign Up For This!"

Living in an anti-pleasure culture — where sacrifice and toil are glorified while pleasure-seeking is disdained — we've been conditioned to *tolerate* unpleasant states like boredom and confinement.

But such states feel bad for a reason: *they suck!*

So if you find a particular aspect of parenting boring or confining, don't tolerate it! Instigate a personal revolution and proclaim...

   "I DIDN'T SIGN UP FOR THIS!"

You didn't intend to *suffer* through parenthood. You wanted to bring more joy into the world. Love and joy: THAT'S what you signed up for!

With that awareness, you can set a new standard. Raise the bar. Don't settle for tolerable unpleasantness. If you can't see a more pleasing way to proceed, just be still, remember your true intentions, and be open to inspiration.

This is not about having zero tolerance for your child. It's not about your child at all! It's about listening to *your* Inner Guidance and *honoring* it.

When you honor your Guidance, it honors you *and* your child.

The Cast Party

As Shakespeare said, "All the world's a stage, and all the men and women merely players..."

Today we'll take that metaphor a step further, for when a play closes, the players celebrate their accomplishment with a *cast party*.

At the cast party, everyone relaxes and recalls the goof-ups, missed entrances, botched lines, and malfunctioning props — not with the terror these mishaps evoked at the time, but with rolling-on-the-floor laughter!

NOW they can laugh because the pressure is off. They've put away their costumes and returned to being who they *really* are.

Here's the wonderful thing about the real-life play called *Parenthood*: You don't have to wait for the cast party to relax and be real. You can "break character" and re-write the script on the fly.

So why not make the play itself more like a cast party?! Why wait until it's over to enjoy the difficult times?

Life is NOW! And it's *all* good.

Driving With the Brakes On

Resistance is like driving with one foot down on the accelerator and the other foot down on the brakes: pretty soon the engine just burns out!

Trying harder (pushing the accelerator) only accelerates the burn-out. But releasing resistance (the brakes) unleashes the engine's true power.

Whenever you start feeling burned out, ask yourself, "In what ways am I pressing down on the brakes?"

For example, say you're trying really hard to prevent your child from getting upset, and it's exhausting you. Maybe you perceive your child's upsets as a personal failure, and you're putting the brakes on that.

Releasing the brakes would mean deciding *not* to resist failing — telling yourself, "It's okay if I fail... It's not the end of the world."

Paradoxically, releasing your resistance to failure would free up the energy you need to succeed!

The Creative Pleasure Principle

Imagine you're in a choir, singing a difficult piece, and it's not coming together. But you persist, and eventually the ensemble achieves perfect harmony, emanating a sound that gives you chills from head to toe!

That's a dramatic example of *creative pleasure*: the feeling of coming into alignment with your heart's desire.

Creative pleasure is a universal principle. It's related to the Law of Attraction, by which similar thoughts and experiences are drawn to each other. As thought and desire come into alignment, pleasure is felt and creation unfolds.

You could say that atoms and molecules "feel pleasure" when they come together to create higher orders of complexity and intelligence. Thus, the Creative Pleasure Principle informs all of nature, from the smallest flea, to the tallest tree, to the human parent and child.

Today, notice that you feel better when your thoughts are aligned with your desires — when you *believe* you can have what you want.

Pleasure-oriented Parenting

Since the Creative Pleasure Principle informs every level of creation — matter, body, mind, and spirit — the most natural way to create a wonderful life is to simply "follow your pleasure."

Being *pleasure-oriented* empowers you and your child to co-create a mutually satisfying relationship. Children are innately pleasure-oriented. They can become "dis-oriented" by the anti-pleasure aspects of our culture, but they readily re-orient on pleasure when we model a pleasure orientation ourselves.

Some parents fear that if they were totally pleasure-oriented, they'd abandon their children! But such fears are based on win/lose thinking. Your Inner Guidance will tell you there's nothing pleasurable about winning at your child's expense.

There is infinitely more pleasure potential in a win/win partnership: "My child and I can BOTH have our desires satisfied... I don't know how, but there *must* be a way."

Today, as you make parenting choices, tune in to your Guidance and wait for the deeper feeling of authentic, creative pleasure before you take action.

WordWatch: Should/Shouldn't

Today, notice your use of the words *should* and *shouldn't*, or any sense of duty or obligation that feels like "a should."

The old paradigm of control through coercion relies heavily on people having internalized *shoulds* — following the rules established by external authority figures.

The new paradigm of empowerment through partnership arises from authentic Inner Guidance, driven by the Creative Pleasure Principle. In other words, the only thing you *should* do is "follow your bliss"!

Pleasure-orientation always eventually leads to *more* partnership, *more* kindness, *more* generosity. Why? Because they feel better than war, hate, and scarcity.

To make the shift, replace "should" or "shouldn't" with "could" and "could *not...*" For example, "I should nurse my child" becomes "I could nurse my child, and I could *not* nurse my child... It's my choice."

Shoulds tend to make you feel as if you have no choice, which breeds resistance — resentment, anger, etc. Connecting with your *freedom* clears the way to feel your Inner Guidance.

The Oxygen Mask Rule

Flight attendants always remind parents that if the airplane cabin loses pressure, you should apply *your* oxygen mask first, and then your child's. This is because a parent without oxygen is likely to pass out before getting the child's mask in place.

Likewise, if you were stressed about some problem with your child, the conventional response would be to focus on "fixing" the child. But stressful states like fear, worry, anger, and resentment are like oxygen deprivation: they undermine your capacity to help your child.

So remember to get *your* oxygen first, literally, by taking a deep breath and feeling for your Center.

Once you're centered — present, connected, "in the flow" — you'll be more creative, and you'll emanate a "vibe" that your child will *want* to align with.

Whenever parenting becomes stressful, stop and tell yourself, "I want to respond from my Heart, so I will take no action until I find my Center."

Fire Drill!

A fire drill is when a fire alarm is set off intentionally so you can *practice* responding wisely in the event of a real fire. When you've gone through the motions repeatedly, your body will "know" what to do even if you freak out and can't think clearly.

Parental anger is like a raging fire that can consume you and your child. But you can predetermine your escape route and rehearse it by doing "emotional fire drills" when you're feeling relaxed and clear-minded.

Start by imagining a frustrating situation until you feel a sense of the anger it might elicit. Then practice whatever technique works for you to transform or redirect the anger energy in a harmless way.

Techniques that involve a physical component — such as deep breathing, whole-body movement, or vocalizing — are especially effective. Have fun with it!

Most importantly, choose or create an anger transformation routine that leads you back to your heart — empowered, centered, and creative — and practice until you can get there even in the heat of the moment.

Falling In Love for the First Time... Again

Do you remember the moment you fell in love with your child for the first time? For some it happens before birth, for some it's the moment of birth ("love at first sight"), and for some love blossoms much later.

For most parents it's easier to love a newborn unconditionally than an older child, because we have fewer expectations of babies — their existence alone is a blessing.

Today, take a moment to recall the times your child has inspired your heart to open wider than ever before. Let yourself re-experience that glorious feeling of Pure Love washing over and through you!

The more often you deliberately re-activate that feeling, the easier it'll be to stay centered in your heart — even under conditions that seem unacceptable.

When you feel your heart closing, simply recall those peak experiences to help you return to your natural state of open-hearted, easy-flowing Love.

Tell yourself often: "Unconditional Love is my *birth-rite!*"

The Power of Humility

The root of the word *humble* means "earth" or "ground." To be humble, then, is to be *grounded*.

As you stand over the ground, the ground *stands under* you. In other words, it "understands" you. Likewise, as you practice humility, you become more understanding of others.

Perhaps the greatest power of humility is that it empowers you to grow. When you're humble enough to admit your ignorance (without berating yourself), you create space for learning and growth.

Always remember that embracing humility is empowering, not humiliating. Humiliation is when humility is *forced* on you. When you're already humble, you can't be humiliated.

Today, if you notice yourself *resisting* humiliation — e.g., when your child "acts out" in public, or when you compare yourself to other parents — tell yourself, "Humility IS Power!" Feel the power of the ground under your feet and imagine yourself merging with it.

Patience, compassion, and creativity come easily when you feel connected to the Ground of Being that understands everything.

Children ALWAYS Cooperate

Parents often feel frustrated when their children don't "cooperate" — when they don't go along with the parents' stated intentions.

Today, no matter how your child behaves, take the perspective that your child is *always* cooperating with you — if not behaviorally then *vibrationally.* Children sense their parents' "vibes" and reflect back a similar vibration, often exaggerated in their behavior.

For example, if your child is impatient, ask yourself how s/he might be "cooperating" with you vibrationally. "In what way(s) have *I* been emanating an impatient vibe?"

If your child is resistant, ask yourself, "Am *I* being resistant in some way?" Look beyond the obvious and *feel* for an answer.

Fortunately, it works both ways, so that when you're feeling joyful, your child will "cooperate" with that, too! But depending on your established patterns of interaction, it may take some time for your child's *behavior* to reflect your positive vibration.

In the meantime, you can practice enjoying Well-Being *unconditionally.*

Unreasonable Love

To love *unconditionally* means you don't need a "reason" to justify loving. In other words...

1. When you have a good reason to love, then you love.

2. When you have a good reason *not* to love, you love anyway.

3. You love for no reason at all.

In our conditional-loving culture, "reasonable" loving is the norm. So today let's practice the second and third types of loving...

Whenever your child behaves in a way that would conventionally be seen as an excuse to love *less*, be a rebel and love *more*! That doesn't mean praising behavior you dislike, it means responding with your heart wide open.

Also, draw a heart on the back of your hand (or create any easily noticeable cue), and whenever you notice it, say "I love you" or offer your child a hug, a loving gaze, or any loving gesture.

How does it feel to love "just because"? Are you willing to love *yourself* "unreasonably" too?

Blessing the Mirror

Today, stand before a mirror and bless it for the gift of reflection...

Thank you, blessed mirror, for helping me see myself, so I can use that awareness to express myself more authentically.

Thank you for letting me see when my face shows signs of stress, so I can shift my thinking until my reflection indicates that I've found my way back to Well-Being.

You know where this is going, don't you? . . .

Your child is the mirror!

When you don't like what you see in your child, there's a good chance s/he's reflecting some aspect of yourself that's out of alignment with Who You Really Are.

Be open to seeing that. And remember that it's rarely a *literal* reflection. Children often reflect their parents' shadows in exaggerated or quirky ways. Follow your intuition.

Bless your beloved "mirror" and focus on being true to your Self. Eventually, your child will reflect that Truth back to you.

WordWatch: My

Possessiveness is rooted in scarcity thinking, which undermines the natural tendency to expand joy through sharing.

We inadvertently teach our children scarcity thinking by overusing possessive words like *my, mine, yours, Daddy's, sister's,* etc. There's nothing inherently wrong with these words, but questioning their use can help us shift into abundance thinking.

For example, imagine asking your child, "Do you want a bite of my apple?" Is the word "my" really needed? Why not simply call it "this" apple?

When ownership is emphasized, it sends a subtle message: "I have control over this." It alters the child's perception of the owned object, making it seem like a source of power. "Your" apple is more likely to become the object of a power struggle.

Today, try to notice whenever you use possessive words, and ask yourself if they make you feel lacking or abundant — like a competitor ("that's MY chair") or a partner ("put your hand in mine").

Letting Go of HOW

Creativity involves exploring the unknown. So if you want to *parent* creatively, you need to accept that you often won't have the comfort of knowing, in advance, *how* it's all going to work out.

In other words, creative parenting is what you might call a "faith journey." You're constantly facing the unknown and surrendering to it. When you surrender to the unknown, you open a channel to inspiration and new knowledge.

Today, if at some point your child's desire seems incompatible with yours, tell yourself that there must be a way that both of you can feel satisfied, even though you don't yet know what that is.

"I don't need to know how... I trust that a way will be revealed."

Remember that the most creative solutions often defy logic!

Your Portable Comfort Zone

Unconventional, creative parenting can be great fun! It can also be overwhelming as you're constantly facing the unknown and stepping outside your "comfort zone."

To ease your journey, try bringing your comfort zone with you, so to speak, by creating a list of comforts — simple, soothing/energizing activities you can do whenever you feel overwhelmed.

Write the list on a small card and carry it in your wallet or pocket. Here's a sample list:

◆ Take a hot bath
◆ Take a brisk walk
◆ Find a quiet place
◆ Sing/Dance with favorite album
◆ Call best friend
◆ Think about my beloved childhood pet
◆ Read *The Daily Groove*!

Be sure to include things you can do with your kids, things you can do away from home, and at least one thing you can do entirely in your mind. Don't list comforts that have negative side-effects. Keep it simple and easy.

Whenever you start to feel overwhelmed, just scan your comfort list and choose the most practical one, given your situation. With practice, you'll find that you can dissolve your stress with as little as 30 seconds of deliberate self-comforting!

Say Goodbye to Guilt

Have you ever had a not-so-good "friendship" with someone who was negative, cynical, critical, or even abusive?

Letting go of such relationships can be hard, but when you have the courage to stop investing your energy in a life-draining relationship, you reconnect with your Authentic Power and start feeling your natural vitality and joy again.

Parental *guilt* is like one of those energy-sucking "friends" you could do without.

So today, notice whenever guilt comes along and starts another one of its negative rampages about your parenting. Gently release guilt by focusing on your true friends: Unconditional Love and Self-Acceptance.

Thank you, guilt, for trying to be my friend.
I know you meant well, but it's not working
for me anymore. I'm done. You can try calling,
but I won't return your calls. Goodbye, guilt...

Hello, Love!

Infinite Love

Everyone knows $1+1=2$. But what is infinity *plus one?* It's still infinity! In other words, infinity doesn't play by the rules of simple math.

To love *unconditionally*, you have to play the infinity game. You have to transcend the zero-sum game that says love is scarce.

You have to question the belief that every time you give love to your child, *less* love is available to your other child... or your partner... or yourself.

Today, practice remembering your connection to Infinite Love. Every time you give from that Love, imagine your "Love Account" balance becoming Infinity minus one, which is still Infinity!

When you drop the belief that love is scarce — that it must be divided "fairly" between family members — and you just follow your heart instead, you'll begin to *experience* that Love really IS infinite.

The One-Body Principle

Suppose your right leg began twitching for no apparent reason. If it persisted, you'd do something about it. You might massage your leg or take some vitamins that support nerve functions.

But you wouldn't yell at your leg or threaten to hurt it! Nor would you ignore it and think, "It's the leg's problem, not mine." Such responses wouldn't make sense because your leg is a part of YOU.

Likewise, when your child's behavior seems unreasonable, you can overcome the temptation to react negatively by responding to your child as if s/he were a part of your body.

Like the parts of your body, your child functions well when you pay attention to his or her signals and, instead of resisting those signals, you do your best to honor and respond to them. There's no blame; you just deal with it.

Today, imagine you and your child are like one body and notice how that perspective affects your interactions.

Your Heart's Desire

Today, simply notice how you FEEL as often as possible. Then note the thought *beneath* the feeling.

Strong positive emotions indicate that your thought is in *alignment* with your heart's desire — you're being authentic!

Strong negative emotions mean that your thought is *out of alignment* with your heart's desire — you need a new thought!

An Example

Your child ignores your request to come with you, and you feel frustrated. You notice that you're thinking, "s/he doesn't respect me."

You ask yourself, "What's my heart's desire?" The first answer that comes to mind is "I want to be respected." But you notice it actually makes you feel a bit worse.

So you go deeper into your heart, and you eventually feel a wave of *relief* when you think, "I just want to *know* that I'm worthy of respect, regardless of my child's behavior."

The feeling of relief always indicates that your thoughts are coming into alignment with your heart's desire. And emotions like love and appreciation indicate total alignment...

Welcome home!

The Body Scan

Parenting in accord with the Creative Pleasure Principle requires the ability to actually *feel* your creative pleasure. Unfortunately, most of us have been trained to ignore or suppress feelings to some extent.

One way to enhance your feeling ability is by doing a *body scan*:

1. Lie down and take a few deep breaths, releasing tension with each exhale.

2. Imagine an energy field slowly scanning (like a photocopier) across your body, from your toes to the top of your head. Your objective is simply to *feel* each part of your body as the imagined field touches it.

3. *Optional:* Repeat the scan, only this time pause at each body part or area and ask it, "What's *your* desire?" Then wait and *feel* for the answer. You might sense, for example, that your toes want to be more in touch with the Earth, your belly wants to be loved unconditionally, and your elbows are just happy to exist!

The more you practice connecting with your body's wisdom through subtle feelings, the easier it is to be a pleasure-oriented parent.

Practicing For Peace

When learning a new skill such as painting, tennis, piano, etc., *practicing* is essential to mastery.

Today, when you're in a good mood, you can play the following "mind game" to practice the *inner* skill of creating peace:

1. Imagine your child doing something that would normally upset you.

2. Notice how you perceive the behavior to be wrong, unacceptable, annoying, embarrassing, offensive, or hurtful.

3. Now pretend it's your first day on Earth and you don't "know" that the behavior is "wrong" and that you're *supposed* to be upset.

4. Deliberately choose the latter, more peaceful perspective and gently release the stressful one. Tell yourself, "I'm *free* to choose inner peace. (Or not.) It's *my* choice!"

Play this game several times, starting with minor annoyances and working up to major "button-pushing" behaviors. You can even make it fun by thinking of ridiculously outrageous behaviors and still choosing peace!

With practice, you'll find it easier to stay centered and peaceful when your child actually "misbehaves," and to respond to your child with compassion and creativity.

Rethinking Sociality

We humans are social animals, and for the vast majority of humanity's time on Earth, human societies took the form of *tribes.*

Modern civilization has undermined our innate sociality in many ways. For example, the "virtue" of self-sacrifice for the collective good defies our natural pleasure orientation.

In a healthy tribal society, where everyone is emotionally *attuned* with everyone else, individual and collective pleasure go hand in hand, for there is more pleasure to be had when one's choices serve both oneself *and* the collective.

But in our society, with its complexity, alienation, and legacy of "dominator" values, it takes an extraordinary kind of consciousness for one to re-create that interpersonal attunement in a way that actually feels good.

Today, notice the things you say and do in order to "be social" — especially around your children and other parents.

You may notice that being socially appropriate — doing/saying the "right" thing, being "good" or "nice" — frequently requires you to be *in*authentic.

For example, in certain parenting situations you may feel social pressure to *control* your child when you'd rather be relaxed and accepting.

$\rightarrow$

Quite often the real purpose of "being social" is to protect others from their own small-mindedness. Such is the case when mothers are pressured to avoid nursing in public.

So being authentic — even when it seems "anti-social" — may actually be *more* social, because it creates opportunities for others to question their limiting beliefs.

When you honor Who You Really Are — *and* you look beyond others' disempowering beliefs to honor Who THEY Really Are — you contribute to the greater good of society.

Today, whenever you choose authenticity over conventional sociality, decide that you *are* being social... They just don't know it yet!

Rethinking Common Situations

Old Perspective: *My children are playing loudly in the grocery store. I should rein them in and make them be quiet.*

New Perspective: I'm serving the other people in the store as I demonstrate how joyful life with children can be when their spirited nature is honored and appreciated. If someone glares at me in judgment, I look beyond their limiting mindset and offer a smile to their "inner child" who would probably love to join my children in play. They also see me using my creativity to be a kind of "buffer," gently/playfully influencing the kids toward expressing their freedom in ways that don't impose on others.

→

Old Perspective: *Some old family friends are coming to my home for a visit. My toddler wants to be naked and my 5-year-old's table manners are atrocious. My guests are going to think I'm raising animals!*

New Perspective: Of course I'm raising animals! Humans are animals with natural inclinations, and by understanding and working *with* my children's nature, and *allowing* them to adapt to the social environment in accord with their intrinsic drive toward belonging in ever-expanding social circles, I'm showing my guests that it's possible to have faith in human nature. They may not fully "get" it until they see my children ten years from now — that somehow they learned to use clothing, silverware, manners, etc., without having been forcefully trained.

Old Perspective: *When we visit the doctor or dentist, my children should sit quietly while we wait for our appointment to begin.*

New Perspective: My children bring lightness and joy even to places where people are in fear. I love thinking that some adult who is nervous about dental work or medical issues might be pleasantly distracted by my little joymongers!

No Problem!

Having a "bad parenting day"?

Whatever you're stressing about — your child won't stop whining... you're way behind on the laundry... the baby nursed "all" night long... you yelled at the kids *again*... etc., etc. — remember there are two components to every problem:

1. The actual condition
2. Your *belief* that it IS a problem

In other words, you don't *have to* perceive the condition to be wrong or bad.

Would a baby see your mountain of dirty laundry as a problem? No, because wee ones see the world *as it is*. They haven't been trained (yet) to pass judgment on Reality, so they don't see the problems we see.

Well, if a baby can do it, you can, too!

Today, try letting go of the idea that conditions "should" be different than they are. Simply accept them...

"No problem... It is what it is."

But don't confuse acceptance with defeat. You can be accepting and still desire change. And change happens *easily* when you're at peace with What Is.

"I Want It NOW!"

The *inner* process of creating requires two things: *asking* and *receiving*. (See page 110.)

People often fail to get in a receiving mode because of its paradoxical nature. To receive what you want, you must be free *not* to have it. The longer you're willing to wait, the sooner it will come.

If your child is complaining about not having what s/he wants *right now*, s/he's stuck in the asking mode. Ironically, parents often exacerbate the problem by saying or thinking essentially the same thing: "I want the complaining to stop NOW!"

To help your child get in a receiving mode, *model* it: get in your own receiving mode *about* your child's receiving mode! How? Simply imagine your child happily anticipating the fulfillment of his or her desire.

As you deliberately enjoy that vision (even if your child is still complaining), you *become* the change you wish to see.

And when you demonstrate the receiving mode often, your child will eventually fall into it with you — naturally and willingly.

The Sticky Speedometer

Some years ago, my car's speedometer developed a case of sporadic "stickiness."

The first time it stuck I didn't know it. I was driving on a freeway, faithfully checking the speedometer at regular intervals, and I believed it was "right" even though my actual speed was gradually increasing!

It didn't occur to me to question the speedometer's "authority."

Eventually the growing difference between what it was telling me and the *feeling* of my actual speed made me realize that the speedometer was stuck — that I'd have to start relying on my *inner* guidance.

It was disconcerting at first, because I'd always relied on the external authority, but before too long I got pretty good at sensing whether I was going too fast or slow. . . .

Today, let your feelings reveal and replace your "sticky speedometers" — beliefs, expectations, and rules that aren't serving you.

When something looks right but *feels* wrong, be willing to question even the unquestionable. For progressive parents, some of the stickiest speedometers are forms of "parental correctness" that started as brilliant ideas.

Ignore the Score

In the competitive mindset that permeates our culture, *keeping score* is all-important. Without a score, you can't know if you're "winning."

But in a creative mindset you can ignore the score. You're playing "just for fun."

Today, notice how you feel whenever you're *evaluating* your circumstances. Evaluation is a kind of taking score that sometimes puts you in a competitive mindset.

For example, if your child were crying and you thought, "I have an unhappy child... I'm failing as a parent..." you'd be turning parenting into a win/lose game in which winning depended entirely on your child!

To avoid such games, first notice how disempowered you feel when you play them, then decide to stop taking score and start thinking of ways to enjoy parenting *unconditionally*.

Paradoxically, when you don't "need" your child to be happy to prove you're succeeding, your child will eventually be much happier!

Detoxifying Parental Guilt

Are you plagued by guilt whenever you fall short of your parenting ideals? Such guilt may seem a natural response, but it's not... It's *cultural*.

Our culture conditions people to believe that their worth depends on their behavior, so that when your behavior is "wrong" you doubt your self-worth, i.e., you feel guilty.

But if you knew absolutely that you *are* worthy of love and respect — *unconditionally* — you'd never feel guilty. You'd simply feel "off" whenever your behavior was out of alignment with your values.

That "off" feeling would be a welcome sign that you need to adjust your course. And with your self-worth beyond dispute, you'd be confident in your ability to get back on track.

So next time you feel parental guilt, say to yourself, "This has nothing to do with my inherent worth — that's a given. I made a mistake, but I can learn from it. I got a little lost, but I'm finding my way."

You "Should" Follow Your Bliss!

Imagine a world with no shame and blame — where it's impossible to be "bad."

Imagine a world where people can stumble, make mistakes, and sometimes even hurt each other, but they are never deemed "wrong."

Errors are noticed, and course-corrections are made, but blame and shame never enter the picture.

In this imaginary world, the word *should* is obsolete. Think about it: the force behind any "should" is almost always fear of being judged (which includes self-judgment).

So, in our shame- and blame-free world, "should" has no teeth, and you're free to follow your bliss.

Fortunately, the things that *really* matter to you — like contributing to your children's well-being — feel blissful when you do them, so you *want* to do them. No "shoulding" is required.

Today, pretend your world is free of blame and shame, so you have no reason ever to "should on yourself"!

Start following your bliss and soon you won't be pretending anymore.

Time-In

The popular "time-out" behavior management technique is less harsh than traditional forms of discipline, but it's still a punishment — like a mini jail sentence. Time-outs usually include a shame component as well (e.g., the "Naughty Chair").

An alternative to time-outs is what I call a "time-in." The purpose of a time-in is not to punish but to help the child get centered and enhance the parent-child connection:

- Rather than being *forced* to go to a time-out place, the child is *invited* to join the parent for a time-in (although "protective use of force" may sometimes be required).

- The parent and child go to a quiet, comfortable place and stay there *together*.

- The parent uses the time-in to get centered and create a feeling of unconditional Presence and Connection, which has a calming, healing effect on the child.

Today, give yourself and your child a time-in just for fun! Establish time-in as a mutually pleasurable activity, not a dreaded punishment.

→

Time-In Tips

Don't wait until your child is melting down to try time-in. Do "practice time-ins" when you think your child would enjoy the connection. And when you're stressed, treat *yourself* to a time-in.

Use deep breathing, affirmations, or anything that helps you get centered. Experiment with different places and ways of doing time-in. The only "right" way to do it is the way that feels best to you and your child. Focus on your state of *being...* Stillness. Groundedness. Presence. Openness. Connecting. Oneness.

When it goes well you might say, "That was a lovely time-in, wasn't it?!" Your child will then associate the word "time-in" with good feelings.

෨ ෫

An extended description of the time-in technique is online at **www.enjoyparenting.com/time-in**

Time-in is most useful for those who've been using time-OUTs and want to switch to a positive, non-punitive alternative.

If you've been practicing creative, non-punitive parenting for a while, you're probably already doing time-in informally and don't need to formalize it.

Why Kids Lie

Parent:
"Did you eat the banana that I *told* you was for later?"

Toddler:
(with banana residue on face and peel in hand) "No."

If children are inherently good-natured, why do they tell lies?

They lie *because* they're good-natured... and they're doing their best to navigate the treacherous waters of a "de-natured" culture.

The toddler is being good-natured when she honors her hunger. It's not in her nature to believe in scarcity, nor to override her Inner Guidance with arbitrary limitations.

She's being good-natured when she meets her parent's *expectation* of wanting the forbidden fruit.

She's being good-natured when she gives the answer she believes the parent wants to hear. It's not in her nature to invite disapproval and disconnection.

In other words, we inadvertently teach our kids to lie when we participate in the Big Lie of our culture: *conditionality.*

Next time your child lies to you, take it as a cue to brush up on the Art of Unconditionality... and appreciate your child's good nature.

Seeing Eye to Eye

As an adult, it's easy to forget how you felt when you were little. So getting down to your child's level can do wonders for your empathic connection.

When you kneel or sit down on the ground close to your child, you see what s/he sees — you literally "see eye to eye." This can be especially comforting for a younger child who normally stands like a diminutive sprout in a forest of towering elders. The move is felt as a gesture of respect and partnership.

Today, look for opportunities to get down low with your child and see a kid's-eye view of life. You can do it to enhance your connection to each other, or to restore harmony when a conflict has erupted.

When you consistently demonstrate that you understand and appreciate your child's point of view, s/he'll be more receptive to seeing yours.

"Scare City"

When you buy into the *scarcity* principle, you live in "Scare City": a place where you're always afraid of coming up short.

In Scare City, you can't enjoy what you have — you're too busy worrying about what you *don't* have. All the cups in Scare City are half empty.

Somehow, young children are largely immune to the distressing effects of living in Scare City...

- They enjoy the abundant *now* while their parents worry about the lack of time.

- They transform their homes into magical worlds while their parents worry about the lack of order.

- They give and receive love endlessly while their parents carefully ration their limited supply.

To live the Good Life, you have to leave Scare City and go to a *dance* — a joyful, magical, healing dance where you release your fears and *shake your booty* like nobody's watching: a-BUN-dance!

Are you willing to do A Bun Dance with your child?!

Pushing Buttons

When toddlers get ahold of computer keyboards, telephones, or any other gadgetry, they go wild pushing buttons! They're driven to discover the magical powers at their fingertips.

At any age, children are driven to push their parents' "buttons" too! Not because they're "naughty" but for two reasons:

1. They need to know what's there — to map the emotional terrain and keep the map up to date.

2. It's an efficient way to get their parents' heightened attention *and* feel more powerful.

When your child pushes your buttons, s/he's doing you a favor: revealing that you've given your power away to the triggering behavior or conditions.

When you de-activate your buttons — consciously choosing to stay *connected* and *present*, regardless of conditions and behavior — you reclaim your Authentic Power! You cease to be someone who can be controlled like a mindless machine.

And your child will lose interest in the buttons you've de-activated, especially if you're also helping him or her find better ways to feel powerful.

The Power of Story

Children love stories for their power to evoke creation:
Stories told with conviction inspire imaginary worlds
that feel real and shape one's sense of truth.

Anytime you talk *about* anything, you are in essence
telling a story that "in-forms" *your* world...

- You tell a story when someone asks you,
  "How've you been?"

- You tell a story whenever you chat with your
  friends about how difficult or easy it is to parent
  your child.

- You tell yourself stories when you recall good or
  bad memories, worry about tomorrow, anticipate
  fun, etc.

Whatever story or theme you repeat most often
becomes the story of your life. In other words, what
you think and say *about your life* becomes *what your
life is about.*

So when some aspect of your life (relationships, health,
money, parenthood, etc.) feels like a *grind*, you can
transform it into a *groove* by changing the stories you
tell about it.

$\longrightarrow$

But it only works if you *believe* your groovy new stories, so it's best to change them *gradually*. For example, if you realize you're running a story like...

"I always get into power struggles with my child,"

...it's not believable to change it immediately to...

"Our relationship is perfectly harmonious."

A more believable new story would be...

"We used to fight a lot, but I finally surrendered to Love — I decided that I'd rather feel good than be 'right' — and now, every day, little by little, I discover new ways to create harmony."

In other words, **you can change your story by telling a story *about* changing!**

Today, pay attention to what you say — to your child, yourself, and others — and ask yourself, "If this were a story, what kind of story would it be? How do I feel when I tell this story?"

Look for opportunities to amend your personal stories in ways that open new paths to your heart's desires.

"I'm Not a Frog-Boiler!"

When you reject authoritarian, coercive parenting in favor of non-punitive, pleasure-oriented parenting, critics and naysayers will warn you that your child won't be able to cope in the "real" world.

The assumption is that "it's a jungle out there" and we should gradually toughen up our kids and get them used to suffering so they won't be shocked when they venture out into the big, bad world.

It's like that famous experiment where they tossed a healthy frog in boiling water and it leaped right out. But if they put the frog in cool water and raised the temperature gradually over several days, the frog would be able to *adjust* and stay in the water.

The slow boil seems more humane, but that "well-adjusted" frog eventually *died* from the heat! Whereas the non-adjusted frog's intact sensitivity protected it from being boiled.

Today, look for evidence that your child's sensitivity is intact (e.g., negative reactions to unwanted conditions) and be *grateful* for it! Tell yourself, "My child will *never* get boiled!"

The Appreciation Game

Here's an *inner* game that's fun to play when you're in a good mood...

The object of the game is to see how many appreciative thoughts you can have without the stream being interrupted by a critical or negative thought. For example:

> *I love seeing my children grow. (One...) They're so committed to seeking joy. (Two...) My parenting groove keeps getting better! (Three...) What?! They're bickering AGAIN?! (Oops! Start over...)*

An unappreciative thought resets the count to zero *unless* you shift back into appreciation right away. The shift back might go like this:

> *Their bickering will probably subside quickly if I stay centered and present... I know they want to get along with each other... They always find their way back to harmony eventually... I LOVE that about them (FOUR!) and I love that I can stay centered even when they bicker. (FIVE!)*

Don't play this game when you're in a negative rut. Play the Appreciation Game to enhance and sustain your *good* moods.

Jump for Joy!

A young girl, having recently completed a growth spurt, is discovering the power in her longer legs by literally *jumping for joy.*

"Can I reach the top of the fridge? . . . Yes!"

"Can I touch the basketball net? . . . Almost!"

Everywhere she goes, she's looking higher, wondering what's now within her reach, and thoroughly enjoying the discovery.

Fast-forward several years... She's trying out for the college track team, doing the high jump. She's competing with several good jumpers for a place on the team *and* an athletic scholarship. They keep raising the bar; the pressure to perform is intense... The joy is lost.

As a conscientious parent, *you* are like a high jumper! Your parenting vision is lofty, and sometimes it may seem the bar is set too high. Those are the times to lighten up and remember that parenting is not a competition — to remember that JOY is the reason you keep reaching higher.

Taking Children Seriously

We live in a society that doesn't take children seriously. Sure, we care deeply about children's welfare; we do our best to help them to grow into healthy, successful adults.

But we, as a society, rarely take children seriously the way they take *themselves* seriously.

To children, *play* is serious business — channeling enormous creative energies and making huge discoveries. But to adult society, it's "just" play, so interrupting or limiting it is not a big deal.

To children, *feelings* are extremely important, not "just" feelings.

If you want to take your child more seriously, don't do it the conventional adult way, which is to assign *weight* to the child's concerns. That only teaches heaviness.

Children take *lightness* seriously. And when you take their lightness seriously, *you* benefit by learning to take yourself *less* seriously!

The Choosing Ritual

This exercise takes a normally <u>un</u>conscious thought process and makes it both conscious <u>and</u> concrete. Don't underestimate the power of that shift — this simple ritual can radically alter the course of your life!

1. Get two sheets of notebook paper and cut each one into eight pieces.

2. On each of the first eight pieces, write a brief description of something you *appreciate* about your child and/or being a parent. Fold them in half and place them in a small container (bowl, jar, plastic tub, etc.). Label the container with a plus sign or a smiley face.

3. On each of the second eight pieces, describe something you find *annoying* or *frustrating* about your child and/or being a parent. Fold and place them in a second container marked with a minus sign or a frowning face.

4. *(Optional)* Decorate each container more extensively with symbols and colors that emphasize the positive/negative contrast.

5. Complete your "altar" for the ritual by placing the two containers side by side in a location where you'll notice them often (or use a kitchen timer to remind you every hour).

$\longrightarrow$

Now let the ritual begin...

Every time you see this "altar" (or the timer goes off), you must reach into ONE of the two containers, pull out a note, and read it. In other words...

You must CHOOSE whether to focus on the positive or the negative.

As you choose, notice that you *are* choosing, and feel the enormous power you wield in that choice. You literally *create* your experience through your choice.

Beware the trap of thinking you "should" choose one or the other; choose whichever one you *feel* like choosing. It's your choice!

Authentic Pleasure Is Priority One

The single most powerful thing you can do to make parenthood (all of life, actually) into a joyful journey is to decide that *feeling good* is your top priority.

It's more important than being right, paying the bills, saving the world, and even being a good parent. Yet when you put authentic pleasure first, you're inspired to right action, you attract prosperity, you make the world a better place, and you're more creative as a parent.

One caveat: the shift to pleasure-orientation unfolds more joyfully when you shift from the *inside out*. In other words, as you reach for pleasure, don't shift your *actions* until you've shifted your *thinking*.

When your thinking is aligned with your Authentic Self, you feel authentic pleasure, and you're inspired to actions that serve the greater good.

For the next few days, pay close attention to how you feel. Notice when you're *tolerating* stress and re-affirm your top priority: to seek authentic pleasure from the inside out.

Are You Your Child's Friend?

"You are the *parent*, not your child's friend!" Herein lies another tragic loss wrought by the either/or mentality of conventional parenting advice.

Why not be a parent AND a friend? After all, a friend is anyone you **know**, **like**, and **trust** — all worthy qualities of a parent–child relationship.

Certainly, we want to be knowable and trustworthy to our children. Being *likable* is good, too, but it's often confused with *niceness*. When friends sacrifice authenticity in order to be "nice," healthy boundaries go out the window. That's the kind of "friendship" you don't want with your children — or anyone!

A true blue friend is one who puts trusting and knowing above liking, so s/he's willing to be totally authentic with you about his or her boundaries and limits. And don't you *like* knowing that your friend *is* who s/he appears to be?

Children who haven't learned our culture's sanctioned *in*authenticity can teach us a lot about being a friend. They hide nothing (knowable) and always speak their truth (trustable).

Whether they can be so transparent *and* likable is up to you: Do you like realness more than superficial niceness?

The Roots of Violence

Nothing is more natural than for a child to become angry when his or her intention is thwarted. Anger is a reaction to perceived entrapment or disempowerment; it activates the body's primal energies for restoring freedom and personal power. These energies can be applied violently... or creatively.

But when anger itself is thwarted — when those energies are successfully suppressed via threats of punishment, withdrawal, or exclusion — the child will descend into hopelessness (relative to the original intention, if not generally). The child may then appear "well-adjusted," but those energies persist, like a sleeping volcano, increasing the potential for extreme violence.

So when you empower children rather than thwarting them, you make the world a less violent, more peaceful place. However, it gets tricky when parents think they have to thwart *themselves* to empower their children, as that can awaken their own raging volcanoes.

Today, look for ways to experience power *with* your child. Be creative. Think outside the box. Give as much as you can and still feel good. And remember that you are not the ultimate Source of your child's power.

The Trickle-Down Theory of Human Kindness

In peaceful "primitive" cultures, kindness is sustained from generation to generation by a kind of "trickle-down" effect. At its core is the commonly held value of serving and delighting younger people:

> Adults appreciate and support the delight of adolescents, who delight in the joy of prepubescents, who enjoy entertaining younger children, who love to carry babies and play with toddlers.

The elegance of this top-down, pleasure-oriented value system is that the youngest people receive the most (and give the least) at the developmental stage when they are naturally narcissistic, while those who give more are more adept at deriving joy from giving.

In contrast...

Adults in our culture often *fear* adolescents,
who call prepubescents "dweebs,"
who disparagingly call younger children "babies,"
who compete with real babies for love and attention.

When your children behave unkindly, remember that you can't enforce authentic kindness. Instead, let it trickle down by *modeling* unconditional generosity. Using your creativity, find a way to serve and delight both "aggressor" and "victim" ...and yourself, too!

The Path of Least Resistance

Take a moment today to observe the motion of water drops descending on a window, windshield, shower wall, or sink.

Each drop follows its own "path of least resistance" toward Ground, which is rarely a straight line. It flows around obstacles in the easiest possible way. When the obstacle is another drop, the easiest way might be to merge with it.

Sometimes the easiest path is that which has been established by previous drops. Sometimes it's easier to stay put until another drop comes along.

In every case, there is no *trying*, no *effort*. There is only ease and surrender. That's Nature's Way. Evidence of this is everywhere — in the growth patterns of wild plants, the movement of animals, and the behavior of children.

Today, set the intention to flow like water through your day and with your children. Notice that when you feel stressed, you're resisting in some way.

And when you feel good, you're going with the Flow.

Are You Resisting Resistance?

As you come to understand that following the path of least resistance brings out your best parenting, your willingness to tolerate inner resistance will decrease.

The pitfall here is the tendency to become even *more* resistant... by resisting resistance itself!

When you say things like "I shouldn't be so impatient," "A good parent wouldn't get angry about that," etc., you're resisting your own resistance.

To avoid that trap, you must be willing to *accept* your resistance even as you choose not to *tolerate* it! Your inner thinking/feeling process might go something like this:

> "I don't like feeling so impatient! (or angry, hopeless, overwhelmed, etc.) But that's how I'm feeling, and I can accept it... It's okay. It's not wrong, it just *IS*. (*...sigh...*) In a way, I appreciate the stress because it tells me I've gone off course and helps me get back on track..."

Whenever you notice yourself in resistance today, deliberately make peace with it. Remember that *accepting* resistance is the first step toward releasing it and getting back in your groove!

Inner Separation Anxiety

Babies and small children often become anxious when they're physically separated from their familiar caregivers, especially their mothers. This instinctive reaction is known as *separation anxiety*.

Sometimes a parent's physical presence is enough to allay separation anxiety, but children feel most secure when their parents are *fully* present: body, mind, and spirit.

In other words, your child may be right there in your arms yet be experiencing a kind of "inner separation" anxiety because you're mentally, emotionally, and/or spiritually "absent."

Ironically, parents often *worry* about their children's anxiety, not realizing that worrying undermines their inner presence, thus increasing their children's anxiety!

Today, look for a correlation between your child's state and your own. Is s/he more anxious when you feel off-center in some way? If so, let your child's anxiety serve as a reminder to practice centering.

Take a deep breath and affirm your intention to be fully present — here and now — at peace with What Is.

→

Transcending Separation

Now let's take this concept a step further and say that ALL separation anxiety is due to "inner separation" whether or not there's a physical separation.

In other words, your child becomes anxious when s/he *feels* disconnected from you, and that feeling may be rooted in *any* type of separation — physical, mental, or spiritual — real or imagined.

If you believe you "have to" leave your child, your belief in lack of freedom will separate you from your Self. Your child will feel that disconnectedness even before you leave.

But when you achieve inner connectedness, it soothes anxieties AND makes it easier to attract into your life more people with whom your child feels a secure, consistent, loving connection. Creating such a "village" can lessen if not eliminate your child's separation anxiety.

So do your best to make peace with separations when they occur, and hold the vision that your child will be okay. But remain open to the possibility that your child can have all the physical closeness s/he desires, too.

WordWatch: "Don't..."

At my daughter's sixth birthday party, I engaged a gaggle of giggling girls in a chasing game by standing in their midst and shouting, "Please DON'T chase me!"

Of course they began chasing me immediately!

Aside from my obvious playfulness, there are two reasons they completely ignored the word "don't."

First, the word "chase" conjured an image of chasing in their minds, and once they *saw* chasing, it was "monkey see, monkey do." (There's no image of "don't.")

Second, they knew I wouldn't have said "don't chase me" unless I *expected* them to chase me. And children are wired to meet the expectations of their elders.

Today, notice whenever you say "don't" to your child...

- "*Don't* wake the baby."
- "*Don't* make a mess."
- "*Don't* hit your brother."
- "*Don't* eat too much of that."
- "*Don't* stay out too late."

What are your "don't" statements causing your child to focus on (and thus attract)? What expectations are you conveying?

Beyond DOs and DON'Ts

If "don't" statements don't work, what *does* work?

Of course, it helps to get clear about what you DO want and focus on that. So instead of "Please don't staple the dog," you might say, "Let's play fetch with Spot," or "Let's staple some paper chains."

Also, ask yourself if there's really a problem. For example, instead of saying "Don't make a mess," you could just decide that messes are okay — a normal part of life... especially with children!

When intervention is clearly appropriate (e.g., the dog-stapling scenario), shifting to positive *words* is not enough, because children pay more attention to emotions than words. So a good rule of thumb is...

*Open your **heart** before
you open your **mouth**!*

With practice, you can get so skilled at centering, emanating good vibes, and conveying positive expectations, that it won't matter what you say... even if what you say includes the word "don't"!

DARE to Be Real!

Older kids often *dare* each other to do or say something funny, risky, taboo, or outrageous.

These dare games give them opportunities to practice being *bigger* than the arbitrary rules, limits, and norms of society. And while the most daring kids may get into trouble with society, they also develop the extraordinary courage needed to uphold society's highest ideals.

Today, pretend you're a kid playing a dare game with *yourself*. Notice when you're on the edge of your comfort zone and dare yourself to step beyond it. For example...

- If your child "misbehaves" in public: "I DARE ME to keep my heart open and respond creatively, even though everyone is probably thinking I should punish my child."

- If your friend is parenting in a way that you believe s/he'll eventually regret: "I DARE ME to tell my friend what I see."

Have fun with this! Start small and build up to bigger dares.

You may find that being courageous makes you feel as big as you actually *are*.

Contraction vs. Expansion

Pretend you're in an acting class and your assignment is to use "body language" to convey any negative emotion: shame, resentment, worry, depression, etc. (Go ahead and do it now...)

How did your body shift? Most likely it *contracted* in some way — tensing, drooping, clenching, tightening, etc.

Now pretend your assignment is to convey pure love, joy and enthusiasm... Can you feel your body *expanding*? Don't those emotions make you want to outstretch your arms like you're giving the whole Universe a hug?!

Your real assignment for today is to do the above in reverse: constantly check in with your body and notice whether you're feeling more expansive or contractive.

Expansion indicates you're moving into alignment with your Authentic Self — you're on your way to bliss!

Contraction indicates you're moving *out* of alignment — stop whatever you're doing and reach for thoughts that make you feel more expansive.

Gradually raise your standard until you become "addicted" to feeling expansive!

The Look

CHILD: What are you staring at?!

PARENT: *(Smiling)* You.

CHILD: Why??

PARENT: *(Continues to gaze, thinking, "Because I
love you so much... I'm just... amazed!
I never knew I had so much love in my
heart... I feel so blessed... I'm so happy
that you're in my life... I just want to
savor this moment . . . .   I want to burn
it in my memory... I want to remember it
whenever I feel disconnected from you,
because this Love is so powerful that
there's no hurt it can't heal! Even if I
sometimes forget, this Love will always
be here... Right here in my heart..."*

"*I will always, always love you!*")

Today — for no reason at all — let your heart bust
open and give your child "The Look."

You need not say a word: The Look says it all.

Re-read the dialogue above and imagine you're the
child — on the receiving end of The Look. Or stand in
front of a mirror and give *yourself* The Look.

Isn't it delicious to be seen through the eyes of Pure Love?

Truth Is Overrated

In a materialistic society, we form the habit of taking objective "truth" too seriously. One of the gifts of parenthood is that children give us an excuse to *relax* about objective truths and revive our natural appreciation of *felt* (subjective) truths.

When a five-year-old boy says, "I'm going to eat this *whole* watermelon right now!" he's telling *his* truth for that moment. If his mother says, "Don't be silly! That melon is twenty times the size of your stomach!" the richness of his heartfelt truth is lost to both of them.

Today, notice how you respond to your child's "childish" statements. Put aside what you "know" and let yourself *feel* your child's truth.

Enjoy the feeling of connection made possible by your willingness to share your child's perspective... Now *that's* power!

Worry Less, Love More

Perhaps you've been led to believe that worrying about children goes hand in hand with loving them. But in truth, parental love is far more powerful *without* worry than with it.

Worries focus all your attention on what you *don't* want and put you in a state of *fear*. This sends a message to your child that you *expect* bad things to happen. And since children naturally tend to meet their parents' unspoken expectations, worries are self-fulfilling prophecies.

Today, use your awareness of worry to shift your focus in the direction of what you *do* want, and reach for thoughts that soothe your worries:

"It's not the end of the world."

"It won't last forever."

"I've successfully handled worse situations."

"We always find our way."

...etc.

Before long you'll start feeling hopeful, and you'll feel your heart opening, too. An open heart is all you need for love to flow unconditionally, unhindered by worries.

The Perspective Game

Think of someone (outside your family) whom you greatly admire — someone you look up to. It can be a friend, someone you've never met, or even a historical figure.

Got someone in mind? . . . Good!

Now imagine you ARE that person. Take his or her perspective as fully as you can. Then imagine that you (as that person) are looking at the actual you.

How do you see yourself from the perspective of this person? (You may notice that this person you look *up* to doesn't look *down* on you!)

Now take the perspective of your child, and look at yourself through your child's eyes. When your child looks *up* to you (literally), does s/he feel like a lesser being? Or does s/he simply feel *connected*? Or...?

Try taking the perspective of everyone you meet today. Have fun discovering the many ways to see the world... and yourself... and your child!

No single perspective is "right." Keep the perspectives that feel good to you, and release those that don't.

Is Joy Knocking On Your Door?

She knocked on the huge palace door. The peephole cover slid open, revealing the grim face of the palace guard. "Who goes there?"

"I am Joy," she answered with a smile, "I'm here to visit the Queen."

The guard shut the peephole abruptly. A few minutes later, it slid open again and the guard said, "The Queen is upset because her children are misbehaving. You may not enter until conditions improve."

"But I bring good tidings, and if she would let me in, the children would surely abandon their mischief."

"Sorry," the guard grumbled, "I must do Her Majesty's bidding." Then he locked the door and left.

But Joy did not leave. . . . She just kept knocking.

℘ ℭ

Today, if you feel upset for any reason, ask yourself this: "Am I using these conditions as an excuse to disallow my natural state of well-being?"

Decide that when JOY knocks on *your* door, you'll let it in... no matter what the conditions!

Power Is Your Friend

The abuse of power in parent–child relationships has a long history. And since none of us wants to perpetuate that legacy, we sometimes feel reluctant to exercise any power at all!

This parental fear of power is at the root of many child behavior problems. It's not that children need to be controlled. (They don't.) It's that *children expect their parents to be powerful.*

Parents who feel powerful, feel secure. And children feel secure when their parents feel secure.

But being powerful is not the same as dominating. Power is expressed most authentically in *partnership.* Domination is power *over,* partnership is power *with.*

Today, look for opportunities to get deeply attuned with your child — perhaps through play or working toward a common goal. Find "the zone" where you're flowing together harmoniously. (You can find this zone by yourself, as well.)

When you get there, feel it fully... That's the feeling of Authentic Power! Memorize that feeling and recall it whenever your child needs your powerful Presence.

The Power of Intention

When you've been feeling mostly positive for a while, it starts to feel *normal.* You begin to think of yourself as someone who "always" feels good about your parenting and life in general. You've got *positive momentum,* which is what makes your daily groove "groovy"!

You can create more positive momentum by being *intentional* — consciously intending to enjoy parenting more.

For the next few days, experiment with setting specific intentions, especially during transition times. For example...

- A new mother going to bed says to herself, "Even if the baby wakes me several times, I'm going to relax as much as I can and savor every moment of rest I do get."

- A father of teens wakes up in the morning and thinks, "Today I'm going to notice and appreciate the kids' creativity and passion."

Set intentions that feel like achievable, incremental improvements. And remember to make it primarily about *you* — not about how your child behaves, but how *you* experience the relationship.

"I Feel Like Screaming!"

As you embrace the idea of honoring your emotions as Inner Guidance, you may wonder, "But what about when I'm so frustrated that I *feel* like screaming at my child?"

First, understand that your Emotional Guidance is meant to guide your *thoughts*, not your actions directly. As your thinking comes into alignment with your Authentic Self, you'll be inspired to better actions. Negative emotions are cues to *go within* and get centered *before* you act.

Second, realize that when you're angry *at* your child, it's only because you've been culturally conditioned to believe that if you feel bad, someone must be to *blame*. And it feels better to blame someone else than to blame yourself.

The key to moving beyond blame is to *allow* the blameful thoughts, but take no action against the "blamee". Take only the "inner action" of reaching for better-feeling thoughts.

If you can't stop yourself, try deep breathing, taking a walk, or screaming into a pillow — anything to redirect the energy harmlessly.

Small Body, Big Spirit

Mother Nature doesn't aim for mediocre. She imbues every child with HUGE creative potential.

Children are born *knowing* they're supposed to be BIG — innately powerful, free, and continuously expanding to new horizons.

Today, no matter how physically small your child may be, notice and appreciate his or her BIGness in spirit.

That spirit is easy to see when your child is expressing pure Love and Joy. But it's no less present when s/he's "misbehaving." In those trying times, remember . . .

Our children are always doing the best they can to stay connected to their BIGness — in a world that expects them to be small.

The Power of Inner Freedom

You live in an abundant universe of endless creative possibilities. So the good news is... whatever you desire, you can have.

The *other* news is... You can't have what you want unless you're free *not* to have it. More precisely: you can only have it *to the degree* that you're free not to have it.

For example, if you want to feel *successful* as a parent, get free to *fail* as a parent. Why? Because if you're resisting failure, your mind is focused on what you *don't* want, and whatever you focus on becomes your experience. (That's the Law of Attraction.)

As soon as you decide that you're free to fail, you stop resisting failure, and that frees your mind to focus on creating success.

The more you feel free to fail, the easier it is to succeed... Go figure!

The Canary In the Coal Mine

Long ago, miners avoided death by bringing canaries into the coal mines. The sensitive songbirds would react to small amounts of toxic gases, thereby alerting the miners to the invisible danger.

In a way, our children provide a similar service. We've been so conditioned to tolerate stress that we often fail to seek relief from it, but our sensitive children have no such tolerance. They often feel *our* stress before *we* do!

So when your child seems particularly irritable and reactive, it's a good idea to ask yourself whether s/he might be reflecting *your* stress. Check in with your body and emotions, and let yourself *feel* what's there.

Seek the fresh air of soothing, stress-free thoughts, and then bless your child for keeping you in touch with your Inner Guidance.

Soccer Field Parenting

I played a lot of chess when I was a kid, and I learned that to win I had to pay attention to all the pieces on the board — to keep the *big picture* in mind.

At school I noticed that when the other kids played soccer, they focused only on the ball and mindlessly *chased* it around the field. But my chess-trained mind resisted the temptation to join the chaotic "clump" of kids surrounding the ball. I paid attention to the whole field and positioned myself such that I could easily score goals when someone kicked the ball out of the clump.

In parenting, children's *behavior* is like the soccer ball, and the majority of parents are like that clump of kids chasing the ball — focusing too much on behavior and missing the bigger picture.

Today, if your own parenting starts to feel like that ball-chasing chaos, deliberately shift your perspective to a more expansive view — the *context* in which your child's behavior is arising. The context includes physical, emotional, and developmental considerations.

When you want your child's behavior to change, and you understand *why* it's happening, you can lovingly address your child's underlying needs and desires, and blend them creatively with your own.

Now *that's* teamwork!

Terrible Two's and Rebellious Teens... NOT!

Q: I thought the terrible two's were just a myth, but now that my daughter is two I'm beginning to wonder...

A: Terrible two's are a reality for many parents in our culture. The myth is that it's *natural* for this or any other age to be terrible. Children rebel only because our culture *opposes* their nature.

When you embrace a "family culture" of creative, pleasure-oriented *partnership*, children and teens don't "need" to rebel.

For one full day, pay close attention to every interaction you have with your child and notice whether you feel like a "boss," a "slave," or a partner. Note that a boss-slave relationship is very different from a consensual leader-follower relationship. The former is domination; the latter is a type of partnership. (Think of dance partners!)

Bottom line: creative partnership feels *better*. Mother Nature intended it that way.

℘ ℭ

Developmentally, toddlers and teens have one thing in common: they're on the verge of a quantum leap in personal autonomy. They're on a mission to become *themselves* — to get in touch with their Inner Power more than ever before.

→

Anytime they feel imposed upon or coerced, that mission is blocked, and they instinctively protest. In nature–based, pleasure–oriented, partnership cultures, such protests are rarely triggered, so terrible two's and teen rebellions rarely occur.

But in our anti–nature, control–oriented culture, parents are expected (if not required *by law*) to oppose or control children's natural developmental impulses toward personal empowerment, which guarantees the terribles!

The shift from terrible to terrific begins with your commitment to creative partnership. Then, whenever your child exhibits "terrible" behavior, you can re-interpret it as evidence of his or her unfolding autonomy, and ask yourself this:

"How can I use my creativity to support my child's growth in a way that works for ALL of us?"

The Myth of Fairness

There's nothing natural about our notions of *fairness.*

If you play checkers with a 2-year-old, he won't perceive any unfairness when you randomly take his checkers off the board, nor would he feel the slightest guilt in taking yours.

Such things don't seem unfair until we are *taught* the arbitrary rules of the game and accept them as "the way things are." Then we feel a sense of violation when the rules are broken: "That's not fair!"

Children often enjoy being "mischievous" because breaking arbitrary rules helps them reconnect with the truth that Authentic Power lies not in the rules but in themselves.

Today, when you observe an apparent injustice, pretend there's no such thing as fair/unfair. It just *IS.* You'll discover that when there's no injustice to fight against, all that's left to do is reach for your heart's desire.

Unadulterated Fun

When parents take their jobs too seriously, they cease to appreciate their children's childlike innocence. They start to care more about being right than having fun. They think they're being "adult," but really they're being "adulterated."

"Child*like*" is not the same as "child*ish*," which is when a child behaves like a caricature of an adulterated adult. Childlike adults seek unadulterated fun: responsible but light-hearted and playful.

Today, let your child's commitment to fun inspire you to relax and be more childlike. And when you're tempted to take parenting too seriously — to "adulterate" — just tell yourself, "Thou shalt not commit adultery."

(Just kidding!)

Leading-edge Parenting Requires Faith

Parenting on the leading edge — nonviolently, unconditionally, creatively — is an act of faith.

There's no guarantee that it will "work," and there's no shortage of naysayers who are quick to tell you it will NOT work.

Blind faith is believing what others tell you, but *authentic faith* is trusting your Inner Guidance — intuition, inspiration, instincts, or gut feelings.

For attraction-based, partnership-style parenting to work, you have to stay checked in with your Guidance, follow it, and accept that it takes *time* for inner changes to be reflected in outer conditions (including children's behavior).

Fortunately, you don't have to wait for those outer changes. You can practice the Art of Unconditionality and enjoy parenting now!

Appendix A

The Art of Unconditionality

Originally published in the October, 2005,
issue of "Transforming Parenthood."

Unconditional love is widely considered to be one of the most valuable gifts that parents can give their children.

Ironically, many parents set out to love their children unconditionally and then feel *bad* about themselves when they fall short. In other words, their self-esteem is conditional — contingent upon their success at loving *un*conditionally!

Some parents believe that giving *selflessly* to their children is proof of their unconditional love. But parental self-sacrifice is an insidious form of conditionality that diminishes both parent and child. Its true colors are exposed when the self-sacrificing parent eventually snaps and says, "How can you treat me that way after all I've sacrificed for you!?"

What gets us in trouble is focusing too much on what we're *doing* and not enough on how we're *being*. The behavior of unconditional loving (what we do) arises from a particular state of mind (how we be), and I call that state of mind **unconditionality**. It makes the difference between superficially unconditional love and the real thing. And our kids can feel that difference!

Let's take a closer look at this concept, starting with a practical definition:

> *Unconditionality* is a state of mind in which you are willing to *allow* Well-Being into your experience... NO MATTER WHAT.

This definition implies that the experience of well-being is always available to you — that you can have more well-being simply by letting it in. There are many people in this world — perhaps you know some of them — whose lives seem to prove this point. They have a high level of well-being *despite* poverty, disabilities, an abusive childhood, or other circumstances about which most people would feel quite *unwell*. But it's not that well-being is somehow more available to them, it's that they are more skilled at achieving the state of unconditionality that lets it in.

Unconditionality is *selfish* in the best sense of the word, because your own well-being becomes your top priority. You give to your child only what you can give happily, and that sets in motion a pattern of giving that continually *increases* your well-being instead of feeling like a drain. This leads to more generosity, not less.

Unconditionality increases your sense of freedom; it never limits your choices. It's entirely possible to be in the state of unconditionality *and* passionately desire conditions to change.

Unconditionality increases your creativity as you deliberately create the inner experiences you desire, regardless of external conditions. So you can have not only unconditional love, but also...

♦ unconditional joy
♦ unconditional peace
♦ unconditional acceptance
♦ unconditional appreciation
♦ unconditional empowerment

And the list goes on... Whatever you want to experience!

An Inside Job

Notice, however, that the list doesn't include "unconditional obedience" because your child's obedience is an external condition.

Unconditionality is "an inside job." It's about how you *interpret* external conditions. It's powerful because, while you can't always control conditions, you can *always* change your mind. You can *always* find thoughts that feel better (or at least bring you some relief) when you think them. And how you think eventually influences outer conditions.

You might ask, "Well, what if my child *won't* obey me? There's nothing joyful about that!"

And I would ask, "Are you sure?"

You see, if you decide up front that you're going to enjoy your relationship with your child unconditionally — no matter what — then what you are actually doing is opening up your creative channels. You are saying to yourself, "I don't know *how* I'm going to pull this off, but I'm open to finding a way to enjoy (or appreciate, or be at peace with, etc.) *anything* that happens between me and my child."

Once a state of unconditionality is well established, uplifting thoughts will come rushing in through those open channels — even when your child chooses not to obey you — and you *will* find a way to enjoy, accept, appreciate, or otherwise feel good about your child (and yourself) in that moment.

But in a state of conditionality — letting external conditions determine how you feel — your child's disobedience would trigger a cascade of negative thoughts:

◆ My child doesn't respect me.

◆ I'm a terrible parent.

◆ Other parents won't respect me if I let my child get away with this.

◆ If my child doesn't learn obedience, she might run out into a busy street!

◆ How is he going to get along in the world if he can't follow rules?

And before you knew it, you'd feel as if your child were about to die or go to prison! Conditions would likely worsen because your child would intuitively feel your fear and negative expectation, and his or her nature is to obey *that.*

In other words, what you *say* you want your child to do is less influential than the "vibes" you are putting out, which can be roughly divided into two categories: *resisting* or *allowing.* You are either resisting conditions or allowing well-being, and you can tell which way you're going by how you feel. Resistance feels bad, heavy, or tense; allowing feels good, light, or relieving.

What kind of thoughts are likely to come to you in a state of *un*conditionality?

- Nothing is worth sacrificing my peace for.
- It's good to know that my well-being is not dependent on what anyone else does or thinks.
- I'm bigger than this. I'm more powerful than this condition.
- My child is reminding me that having control over others is unimportant.
- I appreciate that my child is not a mindless lemming!
- My child is learning to find his own way.
- I love that my child knows what she wants.
- I'm grateful to my child for giving me this opportunity to practice unconditionality.

And so on... Now you are emanating a vibe that your child instinctively knows is the Authentic Flavor of Life. It is irresistibly yummy! And while there's no guarantee that you'll get the obedience you originally wanted, it's a certainty that the quality of your relationship will improve in that moment, because you will have uplifted it unilaterally!

Over time, your ever-improving relationship will make the issue of obedience more-or-less irrelevant. Each of you will be "obeying" your natural desire to enjoy the relationship. This applies to *any* behavior issue.

An "Unconditional Surrender"

I remember a particularly stress-filled evening when my first child, Olivia, was two years old and she refused to get in her carseat. We were on our way home after an all-day excursion and had just stopped at a gas station. My wife and I were exhausted and we just didn't have the energy for a struggle.

But old habits die hard, and I struggled anyway, eventually trying to force her into the carseat. And she — bless her fiery heart — would have none of it! She fought with every fiber of her being to uphold her dignity, until I finally gave up. I surrendered. But I was not defeated; I simply realized that *I* could have a much better time doing *anything* other than fighting my beloved child.

So I relaxed and told her she didn't have to get in the carseat. I decided that I was willing to wait patiently in that parking lot until she was ready to buckle up and go, voluntarily. I told myself, "I don't need conditions to change in order to feel peace *now*," and I looked for something — *anything* — more pleasant to focus on. My solution was to rest my chin on the steering wheel and indulge in the simple pleasure of people-watching — there were plenty of interesting people coming and going about the gas station. (This isn't rocket science! Just reach for *any* thought that brings relief or feels better when you think it.)

Meanwhile, my daughter, feeling the shift from resistance to freedom and lightness, dawdled and tinkered with the various knobs and buttons in the car for about three minutes. Then she climbed into her carseat and let me buckle her in without protest.

I believe this rapid return to peace was, in part, due to the fact that I was willing to wait "forever" — meaning, I was totally focused in the present. In other words, my unconditionality gave her the space and time she needed to find her own way. And with that sense of freedom, we *both* found a way that was in accord with our shared desire for peace, freedom, and respect.

My story illustrates the paradox in which unconditionality leads to positive changes in conditions, but it doesn't work if your intent is merely to change the conditions! You've got to make a commitment to unconditionality for its own sake — because you want the power to enjoy life under *any* conditions.

Our children give us ample opportunities to practice this, and sometimes they persist with undesired behaviors until we get it. It's as if they're saying, "Mom, Dad... I'd really like to go along with you, but I'm going to wait until you've let go of the idea that *I* have to change for *you* to feel okay... I don't want to deprive you of the wonderful feeling of knowing where your well-being *really* comes from."

Unconditionality empowers you to create what you want from the inside out, while conditionality *requires* change from the outside in. When you truly shift inside, you can taste the deliciousness of well-being instantly, and any subsequent outer change is just icing on the cake.

Appendix B

Getting More Support

As you do the suggested activities and processes in this book, and put the principles into practice, you may meet with some inner resistance, uncertainty, difficult emotions, etc. This is a normal part of any growth process — especially one that involves changing your whole worldview!

I recommend you put a support system in place *now*, rather than waiting until you're overwhelmed by stress. At the very least, you can ask a friend for permission to call him or her anytime you need someone to talk to. *(Hint: Enlist a friend who is <u>less</u> stressed than you are.)*

You'll find additional sources of support at my website, **EnjoyParenting.com**, including...

◆ Articles, online courses, and audio recordings on specific parenting topics.

◆ Private coaching support by telephone.

◆ An affordable group coaching program that has helped hundreds of parents create and sustain their own daily groove. It includes a variety of practical support resources, an amazing online community of like-minded parents, and several ways to get personalized support.

◆ Workshops, presentations, and other live events.

◆ Recommended books and resources.

Practicing the Art of Unconditionality means changing "from the inside out," but that doesn't mean going it alone. Sometimes it means making the *inner* decision that you deserve some *outside* support.

~ *Scott Noelle* (scott@enjoyparenting.com)

Appendix C: Alphabetical List of Grooves

The 51% Principle.................97
The Absolute Value of Your Child....64
Acceptance vs. Tolerance.............58
The Appreciation Game.................177
Are You Resisting Resistance?.......187
Are You Your Child's Friend?.........183
Authentic Pleasure Is Priority One.....182
Balance vs. Bigness.......................76
Be Real...................................102
Be Selective... Go Shopping!...........27
Be Self/Centered...........................24
Be Unreasonable...........................40
"Because I Said So!"........................71
"Because" vs. "Be Cause"................70
The Benefit of the Doubt.................66
Beyond DOs and DON'Ts...............191
Beyond Right and Wrong................33
The Big Lie..................................56
Blessing the Mirror.......................149
The Body Scan.............................157
Boycott That Thought!...................41
The Canary In the Coal Mine..........204
The Cast Party..............................138
Children ALWAYS Cooperate..........147
The Choosing Ritual.....................180
Confidently Uncertain...................114
Contraction vs. Expansion.............193
Creative Democracy......................121
The Creative Pleasure Principle......140
Creator, or Reactor?......................48
DARE to Be Real!..........................192
Desires Are More Attractive............92
Detoxifying Parental Guilt.............166
"Do-Over!"....................................82
Don't Explain...............................85
Driving With the Brakes On............139
Easing Exhaustion from Within........81
Emotional Midwifery.....................109
Every Day Is Mother's Day!...........118
Falling In Love for the
    First Time... Again.....................145
FEEL Your Way to Find Your Way......98
Feeling Good vs. Being "Right".......125
Finding Your Groove...
    One Day at a Time........................20
Fire Drill!....................................144

The Freedom Paradox.....................75
From REactive to PROactive...........128
Generalizing Desires......................101
Get In a Receiving Mode................110
Go With the Flow...
    Even If It's 'Wrong'......................28
Going Along for the Ride................83
Goodness Is Inspired, Not Required...136
Growing Down..............................25
Have a NICE day!..........................30
Healthy Selfishness......................113
Helping vs. Co-creation..................29
Hindsight In Foresight...................112
A Human Becoming.......................105
"I Didn't Sign Up For This!"............137
"I Feel Like Screaming!".................201
"I Want It NOW!"..........................163
"I'd Rather Feel Good!"...................32
"I'm Not a Frog-Boiler!".................176
Idealism vs. Perfectionism.............21
Ignore the Score............................165
Implicit Validation.........................99
Independence Day for
    (R)evolutionary Parents..............119
Infinite Love................................154
Inner Freedom Feels Good.............44
Inner Separation Anxiety...............188
Interpret Your Way to Partnership....59
Invisible Abundance......................88
Invisible Teaching.........................36
Is Joy Knocking On Your Door?......198
The Joy of Being Known.................46
The Joy of Manipulation................55
The Joy of NOT Being Known.........47
The Joy of Sharing........................104
Jump for Joy!...............................178
Kids Hear Your Vibe,
    Not Your Words..........................95
Leading-edge Parenting
    Requires Faith............................210
Let Your Love Shine......................23
Letting Go of HOW.......................151
Life Is Messy... Get Over It!...........130
The Look....................................194
The Love Game............................117
Love Notes to Myself....................124

Love the Behavior, Too..................84
Love Train.................................57
Making Peace With What Is.............67
Matters of Life and Death............120
Merging With Your Child's Flow.......22
Mother Nature Always Says YES! 35
The Myth of Fairness....................208
Needs and Desires........................90
No Consequences........................107
No Problem! 162
No Regrets..................................53
Not Wrong..................................54
Nothing but Roses.......................100
The Now Game.............................69
The One-Body Principle................155
The Oxygen Mask Rule.................143
Part-Time Santa,
    Full-Time Visionary..................123
The Path of Least Resistance.........186
Patience vs. Presence...................133
The Perspective Game..................197
The Play Ethic..............................49
Pleasure-oriented Parenting...........141
Positive Apology...........................94
A Post-Modern Thanksgiving.........122
Power Is Your Friend....................199
The Power of an Open Heart...........68
The Power of AND.........................93
The Power of Attraction.................63
The Power of Humility..................146
The Power of Inner Freedom.........203
The Power of Intention.................200
The Power of Silence......................78
The Power of Story.......................174
Practicing For Peace....................158
PResponsive Parenting.................134
Protectiveness vs. Trust.................62
Pushing Buttons..........................173
The (Real) Magic Word..................96
Red Light, Green Light...................52
Relieving Time Pressure...............127
Remember Your Purpose..............116
Resistance Is Futile.......................26
Rethinking Consistency.................60
Rethinking Sociality.....................159
Rich With Desire..........................86
Riding Coattails............................61
The Roots of Violence..................184

Say Goodbye to Guilt...................153
Say Yes FIRST...............................34
Say YES to Desire..........................50
"Scare City".................................172
Seeing Eye to Eye........................171
Seeing the Forest for the Trees......129
The Shadow of a Doubt................115
Small Body, Big Spirit...................202
Soccer Field Parenting..................205
The Sticky Speedometer...............164
Swashbuckling Through
    Parenthood.............................89
Taking Children Seriously.............179
Terrible Two's and
    Rebellious Teens... NOT! 206
There is only YES.........................103
Time-In.....................................168
Transcending Culture.....................65
Transforming Anger.......................72
The Trickle-Down Theory of
    Human Kindness......................185
Truth Is Overrated.......................195
Two Kinds of Responsibility..........126
Unadulterated Fun.......................209
An Unconditional Icebreaker...........79
Unconditional Presence:
    The Oak Tree...........................106
Unconditionality vs. Desires...........43
Unreasonable Love......................148
Weird Is Good! 80
"What Happened?!".......................37
What Is "YES-Energy"?....................51
What Makes Kids So Wonderful?.....131
"What's GOOD about that?".............42
Who's Demanding?........................45
Why Kids Lie...............................170
Why?..108
The Wild Child..............................77
WordWatch: Always/Never............135
WordWatch: My...........................150
WordWatch: Should/Shouldn't.......142
WordWatch: "Don't..." 190
Worry Less, Love More..................196
WWCD: What Would a Child Do?.....132
You "Should" Follow Your Bliss! 167
Your Emotional Guidance...............38
Your Heart's Desire......................156
Your Portable Comfort Zone..........152

Made in the USA
Charleston, SC
18 March 2013